PELICAN BOOKS

EDITED BY V. K. KRISHNA MENON

Advisory Editors : H. L. BEALES, Reader in Economic
History, University of London; W. E. WILLIAMS,
Secretary, the British Institute of Adult Education;
SIR PETER CHALMERS-MITCHELL, C.B.E., F.R.S., F.Z.S.
DR. SC., LL.D., Secretary of the Zoological Society
1903–1935

LIBERTY IN THE MODERN STATE

BY HAROLD J. LASKI

PELICAN BOOKS

LIBERTY IN
THE MODERN STATE

BY
HAROLD J. LASKI

*Professor of Political Science
in the University of London*

With a new Introduction

PUBLISHED BY
PENGUIN BOOKS LIMITED
HARMONDSWORTH MIDDLESEX ENGLAND

First published 1930
Second Impression 1930
Published in Pelican Books 1937

MADE AND PRINTED IN GREAT BRITAIN FOR PENGUIN BOOKS LIMITED
BY PURNELL AND SONS, LTD., PAULTON (SOMERSET) AND LONDON

To
FRIDA AND DIANA

PREFACE

In the summer of 1929 I was invited to give the Colver lectures at Brown University; I was honoured by being able to accept. But my appointment, a few months later, as a member of the Lord Chancellor's Committee on Delegated Legislation compelled me to withdraw from the post. I have thought, however, that the publication of the lectures (a condition of their delivery) might not be inopportune at the present time.

The book must speak for itself. Here I would only acknowledge the debt it owes to many of my friends, and especially to Mr. Justice Holmes, the late Professor L. T. Hobhouse, Mr. R. H. Tawney, and Professor Felix Frankfurter. It owes much, too, to my seminar at the London School of Economics and Political Science, the members of which have dissected it almost word by word. I need not say that none of these has any responsibility for the opinions I have expressed.

H. J. L.

Jan. 1st, 1930.
The London School of Economics
and Political Science.

CONTENTS

LIBERTY
IN THE MODERN STATE

INTRODUCTION TO THE PELICAN EDITION

I

IN the seven years since this book was first published
the condition of liberty has visibly deteriorated over
most of the civilized world. The advent of Herr Hitler
to power in Germany in 1933 is only the most far-
reaching example of a wide and profound attack
upon freedom and political democracy. Constitutional
principle is everywhere upon the defensive. Respect
for international law seems to decline before our eyes.
Racial and religious prejudices which we had fondly
believed to be the outcome of ignorant reaction have
been made the basis of national policy; and learned
men have been found able to reconcile the defence of
this barbarism with their consciences. In Austria and
Greece, in Spain and most of the Balkans, representative
government, in any vital sense, no longer exists; and in
none of them is it likely to revive in the near future.
Even in countries like France there have been moments
when public liberty has been gravely threatened by the
forces of reaction; and if there has seemed a happier
record in Great Britain, Scandinavia and the United
States, no one is entitled to any certainty about the
future of freedom there. At times it has seemed not
improbable that mankind is about to enter a new dark
age. Certainly there are few serious thinkers who doubt
that if the present grave uncertainties in the international field lead to a new major conflict, there is
little prospect that freedom will survive.

What is the cause of this deterioration? A great nation like the German people does not lightly embark upon the destruction of freedom of the mind in every aspect of its social and spiritual life. It does not easily permit a wholesale attack upon religious faiths, the exile of its greatest thinkers, scientific and spiritual, the destruction of its working-class movements, the overthrow of the rule of law, the outlawry of a whole race, the reduction of its press, its educational system and its apparatus of general culture to the level of an inert and mechanical department of government propaganda. It does not, at least with comfort, elevate such a mass-assassination as that of June 30, 1934, to identity with the principles of supreme justice. And in all this Germany does not stand alone. What Mr. H. G. Wells has termed the 'raucous voices' seem able, over vast areas of mankind, to dragoon men to their will. They dismiss freedom of thought as worthless. They forbid freedom of association. The normal rule of law is bent to the service of their arbitrary discretion. They refuse respect to international obligation. They impose restrictions, unthinkable a generation ago, upon freedom of movement. They abandon ideals of social reform and individual happiness in the search, at any cost, for power. They have revived the law of hostages. They have been guilty of cruelties so gross, of infamies so unspeakable, that ordinary men have bowed their heads in shame at the very mention of their crimes. In a sense far more profound than any to which Louis XIV or Napoleon could venture to claim they have exacted an admission that they are the State; and they have compelled a worship of, and a service to, its compulsions unknown to Western civilization since the Dark Ages.

In large degree, their power has been built upon the scientific organization of terror; men will not easily be led to protest when death and torture and imprisonment are the penalty for its utterance. But what has been singular in these times is that admiration for the dictators has not been confined to men who have little alternative but to proffer it. Even in the countries where freedom has not yet been overthrown, there have been found citizens either willing to condone these outrages, or, at least, to insist that they are not our concern. Statesmen of eminence have discovered in these bravos of the new Renaissance men, if not worthy of emulation, at least deserving of our friendship. They have sought to stifle criticism of their excesses. They have dismissed their brutalities as trivial alongside the achievements they have been able to organize. They announce that, in a true perspective, the destruction of German freedom is the restoration of discipline to its citizens. They explain that a foreign policy which, leading the world to a new, mad race in armaments, threatens a new international conflagration, is properly to be understood as the revival of German self-respect. The methods of terrorism which, when used in Soviet Russia, provoked them to war and boycott, they watch without undue indignation as the necessary price of a social order of which, in their hearts, they are able to approve. They are even able to warn us with emphasis that Germany, under the new dispensation, has saved the world from horrors beyond endurance.

The destruction of German freedom is only the most dramatic example of a general stream of tendency which has swept over Europe in these last seven years. Austria and Italy, Greece and the Balkans have had a similar, if less intense, experience. Japan has become, to all intents and purposes, a Fascist power driven by the lust of imperial dominion, and in close spiritual alliance with Italy and Germany. The South American countries remain, with the solitary exception of Mexico, wedded to dictatorship in some more or less extreme

form. And even those countries which still enjoy
political democracy are exercised about its future.
There are significant Fascist movements in France and
Belgium. It is not improbable that the avoidance of a
serious Fascist movement in Great Britain has been
the outcome less of a strong devotion to freedom than
because, since 1931, the Labour Movement has been
unable, or unwilling, to threaten seriously the present
structure of social life. In the United States, a grave
battle is being waged between those who seek to maintain for property an unlimited dominion over political
power, and those who, like the President, have sought
to limit that dominion in the interest of the masses.
What is significant in the United States is the fact that,
despite two great popular victories, the outcome of the
conflict should remain quite uncertain. Not only has
it subjected the Constitution to immense strain, it has
also produced, in men like the late Senator Long and
Father Coughlin, typical examples of Fascist demagogy
whom a slight shift in the political landscape might easily
bring to positions of great significance. It is important
that the central battle in the American scene turns upon
the right of labour to bargain collectively with its employers through organizations of its own choosing; and it
is further significant that, even after five years' support
for labour from the President of the United States, the
outcome of the battle should remain quite uncertain.

Meanwhile, it is relevant to observe that the enact-
ment by Congress of social legislation most of which
has been a commonplace in Great Britain for two or
three decades has brought upon the President a volume
of hatred from the rich unequalled in its intensity since
the Civil War. His effort to make the power of property
subject to social control has opened abysses in American
life the crossing of which may yet involve a revolutionary crisis in the history of the nation.

There are, no doubt, oases in this desert of declining freedom. But nothing so much indicates the temper of our times as the civil war, now just over a year old, in Spain. It is not merely the savage ferocity with which it has been waged. It is not merely, either, that the old privileged classes, army, aristocracy, church, united in a conspiracy to overthrow the democratically elected constitutional government of Spain. It is vital to realize that this conspiracy was hatched in concert with Germany and Italy both of whom were parties to its inception and development. It is vital, also, that when, in an effort to stave off the threat, implicit in the Spanish struggle, of European War, France and Great Britain sought to impose a non-intervention agreement upon the powers, the rulers of Italy and Germany, who accepted it, have throughout evaded its fulfilment; unceasingly they have poured men and munitions into Spain on behalf of the rebel forces. The whole world is now aware that, in the cynical tragedy of non-intervention, the only effective result has been the denial to democratic Spain by the democratic powers of its right as a constitutional government to purchase arms abroad. It has had assistance from Soviet Russia in the period before the signature of the Non-intervention Agreement; and, in matters like medical relief and similar humanitarian measures, it has had the sympathetic encouragement of organized labour in all the free countries of the world. In the ranks of its armies, also, there have fought nobly some twenty thousand volunteers who risked their lives for the cause of freedom. But of organized aid from the democratic states, democratic Spain has had none. They have left it to be the theatre of a carefully planned and deliberately executed Fascist manœuvre, unwilling, at any point, to recognize the ideological significance of the struggle there. An eminent statesman of democratic England could even proclaim that the conflict there was a mere 'faction fight' in which citizens of his own country could take no interest.

II

What underlies this momentous development? Why should a world that had hardly emerged, in 1919, from a struggle announced as the defence of democracy from the onslaught of militarism, find itself, in 1937, threatened with a new struggle in which it is almost common ground that the very idea of freedom will perish? In 1919, it appeared, not less to the vanquished than to the victors, that democracy and international peace had become part of the settled habits of mankind. Defeated Germany took to itself, in the Weimar Constitution, a form of state into which there was written every vital principle of liberal constitutionalism; and the Covenant of the League of Nations awakened the enthusiastic devotion of the common people, not least of organized labour, all over Europe. In the Germany of 1937 there is none to offer the Weimar Constitution even the tribute of regretful memory; and none of the powers today has any confidence that the Covenant of the League is, on a realist view, a serious protection against disaster. Manchuria in 1931, Abyssinia in 1935, have shown only too plainly that those do not accept its premises who were most loud in proclaiming that they inaugurated a new epoch for mankind. Internally, as externally, we have become involved in an intense conflict for power which threatens our destruction. The veiled warfare of class within the State, the imminent threat of conflagration without, these are attendant upon every major item of our policies. Never has economic nationalism been so intense; never has the State control of individual action been so pervasive. A war to end war, a war to 'make the world safe for democracy', has precipitated a situation on every contour of which there is the prospect of war and its twin-sister, revolution. How can we explain so drastic a reversal of all the hopes with which the post-War period began?

This, at least, is certain. Ours is a period of which the major characteristic is insecurity. As always, it has bred in the hearts of men those fears and hates which are incompatible with freedom. For freedom can exist only where there is tolerance; in no other atmosphere has reason the opportunity to exercise its empire. But there cannot be tolerance where there is angry passion, for men in a passion are heedless of argument. There is tolerance only where there is room for, willingness to admit, the prospect of compromise through rational discussion. There has hardly been such an atmosphere in our time. In part, no doubt, that is due to the still unquieted impulse of violence to which the War gave its sanction. A bad Peace Treaty brutally imposed lacked the authority of consent to consecrate its terms. It inflicted a grave blow on the pride of a great people. That blow reacted upon the political régime which authorized its acceptance; and the fact that the régime was economically unsuccessful, that, further, it had never the opportunity to meet its victors upon equal terms, deprived it of the power effectively to govern its people. All over the world the War sanctified violence as a technique of change. It made power, for millions, synonymous with right; and it left, everywhere, groups of desperate men who were determined to carry over into the epoch of peace habits unsuited to the rule of law.

There has been insecurity; and insecurity, as this book has argued, is the essential antithesis of freedom. But insecurity was not born of the War; the War was itself a supreme expression of the insecurity which lay at the basis of our social system. For the War was not the outcome of a deliberately evil choice by the statesmen of any country. It was born of what Mr.

Lowes Dickinson has well termed the international anarchy; and this, in its turn, was rooted in competing economic systems driven by their inner logic to obtain by war objectives they could not reach, or could not reach rapidly enough, by peaceful means. War in 1914, as now, had become the supreme instrument of national policy; and what we have, above all, learned from the experience of the League is that the latter organization cannot fulfil any of its major purposes so long as its members are sovereign states. For the supreme need of our time is cosmopolitan law-making; and the essence of sovereignty is that those who possess it remain, save by their own wills, unbound by the law. This they scrutinize in terms of their selfish interests merely; whether it be tariff levels or labour standards, freedom of migration or the volume of armament, they conceive their policy in terms of the power they deem themselves to require for the objectives, immediate or remote they may be called upon to defend. And those objectives, for the most part, are set by the implications of an economic system based upon the profit-motive. The class in society which owns the instruments of economic power uses the state it dominates to facilitate its access to profit. Its method may be direct, as when Italy deliberately wills the conquest of Abyssinia, or Japan separates Manchukuo by force from the empire of China; or it may be indirect, as when Germany supports General Franco in order to obtain access to the rich mineral deposits of Spain. In all cases, at the base of the complicated motives of national policy, there will be found a drive towards profit by the owners of capital who use the sovereignty of the State to defend the purposes they have in view.

But the international anarchy is, in its turn, merely a reflection of a national malaise. The expansion of industry brought a new class to political power. They climbed to authority in the name of freedom; and they were able to ally themselves with the working class to obtain their ends. The price of their victory was the establishment of capitalist democracy. The revolution so effected meant that the working class was able to use the franchise to exact concessions of material well-being from the owners of the instruments of production. The recognition of trade unions, the right to workmen's compensation, the limitation of the hours of labour, regulations seeking safety and sanitation in mine and factory, systems of social insurance and national education, these, to take examples only, were the price paid by capitalists to the working class for their co-operation in the overthrow of a social control exercised by a landed aristocracy. Broadly speaking, the price was paid with relative cheerfulness so long as the new society was in process of expansion. From its abounding profits, it was able then, without detriment to its security, to satisfy the wants of the masses for an increasing standard of life. The problems of the new society became more complex when the continuance of expansion, by each national state, became increasingly difficult. At that stage, every new popular demand became a threat to privilege. The contradiction between the economic and the political configurations of society became ever more glaring. Capitalism, increasingly found itself in a situation where every advance in social well-being endangered the power of its owners to compete in the markets of the world. It had either to give way before the power of numbers, seeking the democratic ownership and control of the means of production, or it had to move to the suppression of democracy as a principle of life incompatible with its own essence.

The War did not create this incompatibility; it merely sharpened its contours more intensely. Through the Russian Revolution, it established a great national society which stood as a decisive challenge to its own claims. It reinforced economic nationalism, and, thereby, made the ability to secure profit more difficult by the contradiction it induced between the power to produce and the power to penetrate the world-market. The necessity of that penetration, in its turn, involved an immense scientific revolution in the quest for cheaper costs; and this meant that millions of men were thrown out of work and driven, consequently, to look to the State for support. The War, further, had two psychological repercussions of immense importance. It awakened in the colonial peoples an intense aspiration towards national freedom. The result of this was a threat to imperial dominion which gravely sharpened the insecurity of power. The need, moreover, to win the War had led the belligerent states to offer great promises of well-being at its close to the masses. They created vast expectations which, after the War, the masses not only expected to see fulfilled, but for the fulfilment of which they were able strongly to press through the institutions of political democracy.

In the first relief from the pressure of actual war, it is not improbable that men generally felt that a new and generous epoch might commence. The mood did not last long. Reformist governments were costly; they nowhere commanded the confidence of business men habituated to older ways of economic organization. It rapidly became obvious that any serious steps to wholesale reconstruction involved the abrogation of privileges inherent in the ownership of economic power. Those owners were no more prepared to sacrifice their privileges than were their predecessors in 1848 or 1789. They proceded to rationalize without difficulty their opposition to fundamental change. But, in the process of that rationalization, they were driven increasingly to throw overboard the principles of that liberalism they had inherited from the expansionist phase of capitalism. Trade unions become much more dangerous when they were capable of embarking on a general strike. Socialist parties were much more threatening when the masses might be persuaded to entrust them with the direction of the State. Freedom of speech, liberty of association, might then easily mean not abstract argument only, but actual legislation. And that legislation would not only involve a rising level of taxes, certain to fall mainly upon the rich; it would mean, also, the continuous widening of the field of socialized industry, the continuous abrogation of privilege, the growth of an egalitarian society.

The conflict of parties in the democratic state, that is, changed both its nature and direction after the War. Until 1919, socialist parties had either had no representation of any moment in the legislatures of Western Europe, or they had been appendages of Liberal parties, able, as in Great Britain, to exercise pressure upon their quasi-allies, but without the ability to determine policy in any decisive way. The two major parties, whatever their differences, were in agreement that the contours of economic organization must remain fundamentally capitalist in character. Whatever their differences, they were united to insist that democratic government must always so operate as to subordinate its objectives to the acceptance of this major premise. After the War, the Socialist Party found itself, if not the government, at least the alternative government; and since its demands set the pace of political controversy, it followed that, so long as political democracy was accepted, capitalist parties were counselled to outbid the socialists by offering to the electorate costly social reforms as the price of continuing in power. These social reforms, moreover, were reflected in an increased cost of production which threatened the power of capitalists to compete abroad and even, in the absence of high tariff boundaries, challenged their position in their own home market. The result in Great Britain was the recognition of all who lived by owning that, as against the menace of socialism, their area of agreement far transcended their area of difference. They were able to take advantage of financial panic to slip into power. From 1931 until the present day they have used the machinery of the State to consolidate their position. Largely, they have maintained themselves in office by three means. Through a protective tariff (at considerable cost to the export trades) they have safeguarded the domestic market and, in a considerable degree, the imperial market, also, for British producers. They have slowed down the pace of social reform. They have utilized the deteriorating international situation to embark upon a great programme of rearmament which is, in its economic effect, nothing so much as an immense temporary expenditure upon public works. They have, that is to say, temporarily stabilized the position of capitalism. But they have wholly failed to cope with the major causes of its contraction. They remain faced by the alternative of a socialist government intent upon the rapid and drastic transformation of capitalist society.

Capitalist democracy in Great Britain is, at least, something like a century old; and the psychological conditions are not yet present to permit of a surgical operation to remove its contradictions being other than a dangerous gamble. In Germany and Italy that was not the case. Democracy was hardly rooted there; and the War, through the malaise either of defeat or of disappointment in victory had left the idea of democracy without the romantic halo it enjoyed in great Britain. In each country, too, there was profound economic disturbance after the War; in Germany, most notably, the ruin of the currency after the French invasion of the Ruhr wiped out established expectations and destroyed any sense of social security. The rise of Fascism in both countries was essentially the expression by capitalism of its sense that it could not arrest the danger of socialist transformation within the framework of democracy. In each case, a group made large promises to the masses of material welfare based on anti-capitalist action. In each case, also, that group was financed by big business, and made its appropriate alliances with the army and the aristocracy. In each case, again, it proceeded to take power by what was virtually a *coup d'état*. It then proceeded to suppress all democratic institutions, most notably, the trade unions and the socialist parties. All political power was then concentrated in its hands. Freedom of speech and association were rigorously prohibited; terror, which did not stop short of murder even on foreign soil, was used to compel obedience to the new régime. The promised material welfare was, in each case, conveniently forgotten; the new system was, in brief, the unlimited rule of big business acting in alliance with the Fascist Party and supported by the army.

Naturally enough, so grave a change provoked profound discontent; and, naturally enough, also, each dictatorship followed the policy which, as long ago as Aristotle's day, it has been the habit of dictatorships to pursue. Attention has been withdrawn from domestic grievance by concentration on a spirited foreign policy abroad. Italy has followed the path, as in Abyssinia, of imperialist adventure; she has even risked war with half the world in the hope that foreign glory would compensate for a declining standard of life. Germany, without actually embarking upon war, has acted in similar fashion. A great armaments programme has started a race for international preparedness which threatens the foundations of peace. She has attempted to provoke rebellion in Austria. She has (like Italy) withdrawn from the League of Nations. She has sent men and munitions to Spain. She has broken international treaties; and, at least twice in the four years since the advent of Hitler to power, she has brought Europe to the verge of war. Perhaps the best way of realizing the price that has to be paid for this new temper is to remember that Mr. Neville Chamberlain has said that the result of the arms programme of Great Britain is the necessary postponement of social reform for a generation.

Two comments may be made upon this situation. The dictatorships live by naked coercion; there is no way for their overturn short of revolution. And it follows, logically, that since the purpose of the dictatorships has been to suppress opposition to the claims of capitalism, their disappearance will involve the transformation of the economic system in which they have their being. No régime which succeeds them may dare to risk the possibility of counter-revolution. The violence by which capitalism has overthrown democracy is certain to provoke in its turn a proletarian dictatorship which will suffer no compromise with its opponents. Italy and Germany may go down, in a relatively brief period, in war; or, at long last, they may be overthrown as a consequence of the inability of their rulers to satisfy the material needs of the masses. There is, after all, a time-limit within which guns do not appear an adequate substitute for butter. Whatever the occasion of their disruption, they will have left, on both sides, a legacy of hate and passion in the highest degree unlikely to render admissible for a long period the normal habits of freedom. The aftermath of civil war is not an atmosphere in which society can permit itself the luxury of free debate. For such an atmosphere is incapable of the tolerant give-and-take upon which liberty depends. It is a function of that ability to compromise which depends in a society upon unity about fundamentals. It is the tragedy of dictatorship that it does not breed that unity as it moves to its destruction.

A capitalist democracy, like Great Britain or the United States, in each of which the democratic tradition has deep historic roots, is clearly in a different position from countries in which, like Germany and Italy, it was both novel and fragile. Peoples do not easily part with psychological habits of any profundity. Yet it would be a dangerous prophecy to urge that either will escape easily the fate that has attended dictatorial countries. About nothing does passion accrete so strongly as about matters of economic constitution. It is not without significance that, in Great Britain and the United States, hatred of, and affection for, the Soviet Union has been largely a matter of economic status. It is highly significant that both were impelled to seek the overthrow of the Soviet Union in the first years of its existence without having any such impulse in the case of Germany or Italy, that neither has felt any obligation to assist the democratic government of Spain. It is important, also, that in both of them the forces of capitalism are highly integrated, that they have the self-confidence which comes from the absence, so far, of serious challenge to their authority. Yet, in each of them, capitalists remain in a state of nervous tension. Though all the main instruments of power and propaganda are in their hands, they are less able than at any time since the close of the Napoleonic wars to discuss the issues in dispute with calmness. In England, ministers of the Crown have openly stated that a Labour victory would be followed by a deliberate organization of a flight of capital abroad; though they must have known that the coincidence of a Labour government with financial panic was the worst possible harbinger of peace. The attitude of men like Lord

Salisbury, who consciously demand a reinforcement of the already great powers of the House of Lords to mitigate the danger of a socialist victory carries with it its own plain lesson. Others in authority have even argued that the veto of the Crown might be revived as a weapon in the conflict with the Labour Party. And to all this there must be added the temper indicated by the Trades Disputes Act of 1927—the first legislation hostile to trade unionism since 1799—the Incitement to Disaffection Act of 1934, the militarization of the police, the savage sentences—perhaps the most savage since Tolpuddle—inflicted on the Haworth miners, the imprisonment of Mr. Tom Mann for refusal to find securities against a disturbance for which, had it occurred, he would not have been responsible. That it has been necessary to create in these last years a special body to watch against the invasion of civil liberties, and that this body should have been amply occupied since its foundation, is a significant symptom of the times. It is not, I think, untrue to say that the basis of Lord Baldwin's plea to the citizens of this country on behalf of our historic freedom has been his insistence that nothing be done to disturb the confidence of those who believe that its democracy must remain capitalist in character.

In the United States, the dramatic experiment of President Roosevelt has made the inner conflict between capitalism and democracy more overt in character than it has been in Great Britain. There has been nothing of socialist innovation in his measures; without exception, they have been examples of liberal legislation such as men like T. H. Green and Hobhouse regarded as principles of elementary prudence. What is remarkable about them is not merely the volume of hate they have evoked from members of the possessing class, though that is remarkable enough. What is remarkable, rather, is the revelation they have involved of the habits of

American capitalists when their record as the controllers of the national wealth is examined. It is not an exponent of socialism but so eminent an economist as Mr. Keynes who writes of the habits of Wall Street that 'when the capital development of a country becomes the by-product of the activities of a casino, the job is likely to be ill-done'. Anyone who reads the record of the American labour spy, of the activities of the hired armies of thugs normally employed by business men in industrial disputes, of the gigantic scale upon which tax evasion is practised by eminent financial leaders, of the opposition of college presidents and Cardinals of the Church to such elementary decencies as the prohibition of child labour, will wonder exactly what habits American capitalism will display if and when its authority is seriously challenged. And to all this must be added the grim fact that, for four years at least, of President Roosevelt's tenure of office, the Supreme Court has acted as nothing so much as an annexe of Wall Street, 'I cannot believe', wrote Mr. Justice Holmes in 1930 of the way in which the Court treated the Fourteenth Amendment, 'that the amendment was intended to give us carte blanche to embody our economic or moral beliefs in its prohibitions'. But the habits of the Court, in its handling of the 'New Deal' legislation seemed to suggest that the main intent of the Constitution was an authority to its judges to treat Congressional Statutes in accordance with the 'economic or moral beliefs' of five out of its nine members. The Supreme Court, since 1932, has been the chief hope of American reaction; and all attempts to modernize the economic meaning of the Constitution founder upon the rock of the prejudices of its temporary majority.

The stark fact is that so long as, both in Great Britain and in the United States, capitalism was in a prosperous condition, the harmonization of its inner principle with the logic of democracy was no difficult matter. The

forces of production were in accord with the relations
of production. There was respect for liberty because
there was no irresolvable conflict between the demands
of property and the interests of society. But so soon
as that conflict came, so soon, even, as it threatened, the
inherent contradiction between capitalism and democracy
became apparent. The owners of the instruments of
production, there as elsewhere, are not prepared to
surrender the privileges dependent upon ownership. If
democracy stands in the way, for them it is so much
the worse for democracy. They revive against it all the
artillery of argument by which they were so unimpressed
in the epoch of capitalist expansion. The liberties of
democracy, they say, mean a threat to law and order.
They threaten the triumph of ignorant mediocrity. They
put power in the hands of the unsuccessful. They mean
inefficiency, corruption, licence. They contradict the fundamental laws of social organization. The 'revolt of the
masses' is a defiance of the necessities of civilized life.

All of these are, of course, no more than the rationalizations of passion in a panic. But do not let us forget
that they are the rationalizations of a panic at once
convinced and armed. Mr. Ford's hostility to organized
labour, however ignorant, is sincere. And behind men
like Mr. Ford there are not only the great army of
owners to whom the passion for property is the supreme
religion; there are also the men like Mr. Hearst and
his English analogues to whom victory is more important
than peace. In any society they are aware that their
ruthless disregard of principle will leave their own liberty
unimpeded. In a conflict they believe they will win;
and they prefer conflict to the alternative of abdication.
They are not prepared for acceptance of Matthew
Arnold's admonition: they cannot make the sacrifice
involved in the choice of equality and the flight from
greed. If democracy will not tolerate much longer the

poverty and unemployment—much of it needless poverty and needless unemployment—which Mr. Keynes has told us is 'rightly associated with present-day capitalistic individualism', then they are prepared for the destruction of democracy. No doubt they will regard that destruction as a *saeva necessitas*. They will represent the demands of socialism as incompatible with the national welfare. They will be saving the people from itself. They will be adopting outworn and inefficient institutions to the needs of a new time. Perhaps they will argue, like Lord Eustace Percy, that the masses are too preoccupied with political and economic questions; in a new dispensation they can use the energy liberated from that preoccupation for higher spiritual matters. Whatever the basis upon which they justify their action two primary facts will remain. The working classes will have been deprived of the institutions by and through which they have defended their standard of life; and the coercive power of the State will remain, as it is today in Italy and Germany, wholly at the disposal of the possessing class. And it will be necessary, in order to defend the new dispensation, to deprive its critics of the right freely to persuade their fellows that the democratic way is a better road to salvation. For any people that has once enjoyed even a partial opportunity to affirm its own essence can only be driven by coercion into the acceptance of silence.

Fascism in Great Britain and America may come in diverse ways. It may arrive as the slow outcome of an almost imperceptible system of limitations upon public liberty, an accumulation of suppressions no one of which, at the time, is adequately seen in its full perspective. Or it may come as an attempt by a reactionary government to forestall what appears to be the inescapable victory of their opponents at the polls. It may come because of the necessities of national organization in a great war; or out of its aftermath in the attempt to deal with problems of discontent otherwise deemed insoluble. It might even come as a deliberate challenge to a government of the left that had acceded to power; we know only too well from our experience in Ulster in 1913–4 that when men's ultimate convictions, as they deem them, are at stake, the temptation to fight rather than to give way is well-nigh irresistible. After all, a thorough-going socialist victory in either country would mark an epoch in the history of the world. It would change so decisively the balance of social forces, if it were adequately implemented in action, as to rank with the two or three major events in the records of civilization. It would deprive of economic privilege a class that has never known what it is to live in an equal world—a class, too, that has been taught by all its experience that its private good is identical with the public welfare, and has remained steadfastly unconvinced by the scepticism displayed by those excluded from the privileges it has enjoyed. It is a class which dominates the courts, the civil service, and the defence forces of the modern state. Overwhelmingly, also, it controls all the techniques for influencing opinion. It is compact, well-organized, and conscious of its power; it is aware, also, of the deep differences which divide the forces of its opponents. Sincere in the conviction that the maintenance of its authority is necessary in what it believes to be the public interest, is it surprising that it should view with horror the advent of a socialist democracy? And, on all our past experience, would it not rather be surprising that its members should refuse to abdicate when they believe that they have the prospect of victory? No such class in the past, at least, has voluntarily parted with the right to dominate the state-power.

We need not be moved by the argument that there is no evidence of a will to fight. On the eve of the Civil

War in Great Britain three hundred years ago careful observers were insistent that the very idea of sedition was dead. We need not, either, be moved by the insistence that, in either country, compromise is in the genius of the people. National behaviour is adapted to the stress of circumstance. The 'mystic, dreamy Slav' whom we were taught to admire from 1914 to 1917 has become a grim realist, hard, practical, growingly efficient, utterly unlike the stereotype to which past experience had accustomed us. No virtues seemed more deeply rooted in the German people than respect for science and learning; they have not only vanished overnight; they have been replaced by a public veneration for the mystic ravings of a group of gangsters comparable only with the adulation heaped by the Roman mob upon the compositions of Nero. We need not deny the force of any national tradition; we need only remember that national traditions are shaped by the experience men encounter. Where they are formed by fear and hate, the power of reason to determine their substance is necessarily limited in its application.

Let us admit that the tradition of democratic self-government in Great Britain and America is more firmly rooted than elsewhere. On historic experience that does not mean that the tradition cannot be transformed; it means only (let us hope) that its defenders will give a good account of themselves if they are challenged. But that implies, once more, either the possibility of conflict, or that the possessors of economic power will shrink from its implications. Involved in the first alternative is the certainty that liberty, in any meaning sense, can hardly hope to survive. Germany and Italy, Austria and Spain, remain to prove that grim hypothesis. And the one thing that may persuade the capitalist class to self-sacrifice is the persuasion that a challenge to democracy is a gamble too great for it to embark upon. The condition of that persuasion is, so far absent. It means such a unity of the Left forces in the State as will leave the chances of a capitalist victory at the best wholly uncertain and, at the worst, minimal. I do not argue for a moment that such unity is unattainable. In the face of grave danger to democracy that unity was achieved in France, and, so far at least, it has proved adequate to the preservation of the traditional forms. We must not, indeed, build too much upon the French example. What it has secured is a breathing-space for the Left, rather than a transformation of class-relations. It has preserved the contours of French capitalist democracy; but that has been upon the condition that there was no major adventure in socialism attempted under the partnership. No doubt the gain therein is real. But it means that the forces of French capitalism have not yet been put to the supreme test; and it is notable that M. Blum accepted defeat at the hands of the Senate—a rare thing under the constitutional conventions of the Third Republic— rather than risk the consequences of freeing the popular will in France from sabotage by the effete Upper Chamber. The French Popular Front has secured a breathing space for capitalist democracy and the importance of that achievement is beyond question. It has still, however, to be proved that it has built a road through which the French people may pass to the socialization of economic power.

I think it probable that the achievement of such unity in Great Britain might, if it were done quickly enough, and a major war did not supervene, have the same beneficial results for democracy that it has had in France. Here, as there, it would capture political power; and here, as there also, it would put the forces of economic reaction upon the defensive. That would, in itself, be an immense gain for freedom. For not only would it exhilarate the forces of progress all over the world. It would put an end to the war of attrition that Fascism has been waging against international democracy. It would renovate the League, and revivify the principle of collective security. Instead of a policy of piecemeal surrender to the Fascist powers, as in Manchuria and Abyssinia and Spain, it would present them with a challenge to aggressive action fairly certain to change for the good the balance of our civilization. The mere fact of its achievement, moreover, would give new hope to the men and women in the Fascist countries who are now crushed down by the weight of its coercive terror. We are entitled to believe that the renovation of the democratic spirit in Great Britain would be followed by its revival all over Western Europe.

If it is done in time; that is the incalculable element in all our equations. We do not deal with a static world; we cannot measure our forces in terms of the inevitable gradualness of geological epochs. A major war, a new industrial depression like that of 1929, some further Fascist victory on the European continent, might easily destroy the prospect of unity before men see the urgency of its consummation. What is disturbing in the British situation is the complacency among parties of the Left about a situation that is critical. Most of their members seem to assume that here, at least, things will amble on in the old wonted way. They refuse to see the depth of the crisis in which we have become involved. They mutter that it cannot happen here with the same easy confidence that persuaded German socialists before 1933 that Hitler was a merely passing phenomenon. There is, perhaps, a half-conscious defeatism, also, in their attitude. For they have been warned so often by the forces of the Right that militancy on their part is a strategy of disaster, that they tend to accept a plan of battle dic-

B

tated to them by their opponents. The result is to make
them at all costs anxious to avoid a policy those opponents may interpret as a challenge. They watch, that
is to say, the slow deterioration of their position (in
which the status of liberty is necessarily involved) without being able to arrest it. Their assumption seems
to be that respectable behaviour on their part will
eventually bring them to power. They do not seem
to understand that such 'respectability' merely confirms
their opponents in their belief of socialist weakness,
that in politics, as in war, the road to victory lies in
taking the offensive. For the policy of 'respectability'
does not convince the opponents of socialism that its
danger is any less as a doctrine than they suppose;
and it has the unhappy effect of reducing its supporters
either to apathy or despair. The real comment on the
policy of 'respectability' is the declining interest in
national politics as evidenced by the polls in the by-
elections since 1935. That declining interest is a measure
of waning faith in party politics; and that waning faith
is exactly the atmosphere in which the temper of Fascism
most easily grows.

Party government, as Bagehot said, is the vital
principle of representative government. As soon as an
electorate loses faith in that principle the way lies open
to the suppression of democratic government. For
such a lack of faith indicates a belief in the people that
a change of government cannot effectively alter their
situation. Such a mood of apathy is a constant temptation to listen to the 'strong man' who promises, granted
the abolition of parties, the immense improvements
that Hitler and Mussolini promised before their advent
to power. He explains that the old system is outworn.
He insists that it is the principle of opposition which
stands in the way of thorough-going and wholesome
changes. He makes promises to everybody of every-

thing if only he is allowed to cleanse the Augean stables. He exploits every felt grievance to make his appeal attractive. It is the insecurity of employment, the bondage of interest, the foreigner, the big stores, the Bolshevist agitator, or what you will. Since most men are private men, who feel only in a dull way that, somehow, something is wrong, they begin to give heed to the promised dispensation. A time comes when they are persuaded that things can hardly be worse, and may well be better, under the new régime. They run, as Rousseau said, to meet their chains. It is not until it is too late that they recognize that the promised freedom is, in fact, but a more evil variant of the old bondage.

Anyone who examines the history of the rise of Mussolini or Hitler to power can confirm this diagnosis for himself. He will find a constant pattern underlying the whole process. The dictator works on the sense of unease, of anger, of apathy and despair. He promises a new heaven and a new earth. He attributes their absence to a few easily identified enemies, whether men or principles. He so defines his remedies that the average man recognizes in them at least the language of ideas he has been taught to admire. He hears of the demagogue's charity; he witnesses his dramatic parades; he reads of his flaming denunciation of evils he himself abhors. The farmer fastens upon the promise that he will be relieved from tithe. The small shopkeeper is entranced by the vision of a world in which there are no chain-stores and no co-operative societies. The working-man learns that he may be released from the haunting fear of unemployment by the prohibition of foreign imports. All this, to the accompaniment of wholesale invective, passionate drama, well-organized martyrdoms, high pressure emotionalism, gives the idea of a great activist movement, persecuted by the 'old gang', representative of youthful vigour which seeks, despite the power of vested interest, to break through the ancient ways. Successfully rehearsed, it begins not unplausibly to sound to many like a Katharsis for the discontents they vaguely feel without being able to articulate them into terms of rational argument. An affirmation made with sufficient constancy begins to seem true. Invective sufficiently repeated tends to persuade men that perhaps there is something dubious about the 'old gang'. Youth is attracted to the movement because it appears to offer a theatre of action, and because its very novelty seems like emancipation from that older generation whose authority it resents. For men who are bewildered and unhappy Fascism offers the anodyne that religious revivalism has so often brought. It is the supreme release from the gnawing canker of thought.

They do not see—they are carefully prevented from seeing—behind the façade of the demagogue's appeal to the little man, the carefully organized threads which bind him to the interests of reaction. The shows have to be paid for; but the balance-sheets are not published, and the contracts are sealed in private. Neither Hitler nor Mussolini allowed the world to penetrate that twilight in which their real purposes were determined in concert with the vested interests of reaction. These pay the piper; and they refrain from calling the tune only until his misguided adherents have placed the demagogue in power. Only then is the mask of Fascism lifted. The free trade unions disappear; the socialist parties are suppressed; the co-operative movement is 'taken over'. There is no longer a free Press. Strikes become illegal. Critics have a way of disappearing into jail or concentration camps. The 'revolution', it is announced, is accomplished. But the same interests remain in authority after the 'revolution' as before it. All that has effectively changed is the ability of the ordinary citizen to oppose his will to the orders of the government. He has ceased to be a free citizen. Whatever his thoughts, his only right, as the new dispensation becomes effective, is the right to applaud the men who have forged his chains.

III

This is the danger that confronts us in our time; and there is no answer to that danger save the courage to organize against it while there is time. I say the courage to organize against it; for in our day, not less than in that of Pericles, the secret of true liberty remains courage. We acquiesce in the loss of freedom every time we are silent in the face of injustice. The more we insist that it is not our concern, the easier we make the demagogue's task. For it is of the essence of liberty that it should depend for its maintenance upon the respect it can arouse in humble men. Their power to maintain it lies in their willingness to organize themselves for its maintenance. It has no foe more subtle than their sense of apathy or helplessness. And men who have known what liberty means will not surrender it if they are awakened to its danger. Their weakness lies in their inability to penetrate beneath the mask its enemies assume. They have been habituated to obedience. They have not been schooled to read the lesson of the historic movement. The economic interdependence of the world, the necessary relation of boom and slump in capitalism, that system's requirement of an army of unemployed, the degree to which methods of production must shape the forms of the political system to the requirements of their own immanent logic, these things are not the staple intellectual diet upon which they are fed. Most of them are born to live and die without a glimpse of any of the forces by which the world is moved. They have to judge its governance only as they faintly descry the larger context in which its own vast secular changes impinge on their petty lives. Before them is the daily need to live, the exacting toil of work, the need for play and sleep and a brief hour of love. They are schooled to obedience by the rigorous discipline of their lives. It is no easy task to give them the sense of grave dangers to be arrested, of big ideas which need an army to fight for them. Only great leadership can strike their imagination into that action which responds to the call.

The first necessity of that leadership is recognition of the situation we occupy. It is not enough to know that we live in dangerous days; it is above all urgent to recognize the nature of the danger. It is not enough, either, to insist upon the insecurity of the times; it is fundamental to recognize the nature of the insecurity. Our danger and our insecurity are no different in their ultimate causation from the danger and the insecurity which brought about the collapse of Greek and Roman civilizations. We have come to the end of an economic system exactly as they came to an end. Our relations of production contradict the forces of production exactly then as now. What distinguishes our position from that of our predecessors is the greater knowledge we have of the dynamics of social change. We are able, as the Greeks and Romans were not able, to become the masters of our social destiny if we so will. The means of a new and fuller security lie at our disposal, and, with its advent, the means, also, of a new and fuller liberty. For what has characterized our liberty in the past, in almost every significant field, has been its limitation by the implications of the economic system under which we have lived. Liberty for us has been always hindered and hampered by its necessary subordination to the claims of property. It has been enjoyed only as its exercise has not threatened the owners of economic power. Now that the consequences of their ownership risk once more the foundations of civilization, they seek to abandon liberty that they may preserve their privileges. If we permit its abandonment, at some stage, conflict is certain. For the mind of man cannot, in the long run, be habituated to tyranny; at some stage, the slave revolts against his master.

They seek to abandon liberty; and they will succeed unless we organize ourselves to prevent their success. I do not for one moment underestimate the risks or the difficulties of the task. To transform the ultimate economic foundations of society is the most hazardous enterprise to which men can lay their hands. It touches habits more profound, prejudices and convictions more sincerely held, than any other form of social change. It can never be effected without the pain and disappointment that invariably accompany the failure of established expectations. Perhaps, even, it cannot be accomplished save at the price of violent conflict between man and man.

The alternatives before us are stark. Either we must acquiesce in the maintenance of an economic system which, day by day, brings war and Fascism nearer as its inevitable price, or we must seek to change the system. There is no remedy now for our ills save, with all its intricate complexities, the planned production of our economic resources for community consumption. This means—let us face the fact—that the private ownership of the means of production must go. With them must go, too, that class-structure of society with all the privileges it has annexed to the system of ownership it has maintained. It is possible, though I do not think it likely, that if we organize for this end in time, we may persuade men, because the initiative which comes with the possession of State power is in our hands, peacefully to acquiesce in this transformation. Certainly if we are successful in that persuasion we shall have accomplished the most beneficent revolution in the history of the human race. It is, on the other hand, possible

that the privileged will fight rather than give way. In
that event, because we are organized, there is at least
the chance of victory. Acquiescence, in any case, is
only a postponement of conflict. To organize the unity
of those who seek the new social order is, at the worst,
to give them a fighting chance.

And it cannot be too strongly emphasized that those
who seek the new social order are in this hour soldiers
in the army of freedom. They alone can end the exploita-
tion of man by man. They only have it in their power
to establish a society in which there is recognized to
be either an equal claim upon the common good or
differences in return to claims rationally justified by
their ability to augment the sum of the common good.
Our present economic system cannot display these
characteristics. 'The reward', said John Stuart Mill
of its working, 'instead of being proportioned to the
labour and abstinence of the individual is almost in
an inverse ratio to it; those who receive the least labour
and abstain the most.' A society like ours can be secure
only as its foundations permit of its continuous expansion; it is now decisively clear that the age of its expansion
is ended. With its contraction, it is unable to satisfy
progressively the wants of men, and it is therefore
deemed, by all excluded from its privileges, an irrational
and unjust society. As such, it is incapable of the
security which, as this book has argued, is the basic
condition of freedom.

Not only so. The greater the effort to restore its
security upon its present foundations, the greater the
attack upon freedom that is involved. For the way to
that restoration lies through the suppression of all the
instrumentalities of freedom. Its method is depicted
for us by the experience of the Fascist countries; they
achieve security by transforming their societies into
prisons. Science and art are no longer free creations

there of the human mind; they are the instruments of the authority that coerces men into obedience. To seek security, they are compelled to deny their own cultural heritage; and a new and more terrible inquisition presides over the thoughts of men. Yet, even so, they do not achieve security even at the terrible price they seek to pay for it. For not only, in the very shadow of the prison-house itself, do brave men and women arise to challenge its authority—Matteotti and Roselli in Italy, Dimitrov and Thälmann in Germany; it cannot meet the challenge all social systems have to meet—the need so to develop its resources that it can progressively advance the standard of its people's life. In the long run, though, indeed, the run may be very long, war and circuses are no substitute for bread and the free life of the human spirit. Men, in the end, come to recognize this; and, when the recognition dawns, they renew their courage to shake off their chains.

That, let us add in conclusion, is the essential truth behind the grim struggle of these last twenty years in the Soviet Union. It has been part of the strategy of the enemies of freedom in part to decry the accomplishment of its makers, and in part to declare that the price is too heavy for the end. It is vital for those who care for freedom to maintain a proper perspective in this matter. The Soviet Union has been the pioneer of a new civilization. The conditions upon which it has begun the task of its building were of unexampled magnitude in our experience. Its leaders came to power in a country accustomed only to bloody tyranny, racked and impoverished by unsuccessful war. Their peoples were overwhelmingly illiterate, and untrained to the use of that industrial technology upon which the standards of modern civilization depend. They began their task of construction amidst civil war and intervention from without, amid famine and pestilence. For the first years of their existence they lived, quite literally, in a state of siege. They could not have coped with the gigantic problems they confronted unless they had governed in the terms suitable to a state of siege. They were insecure in the two fundamental senses not only that they had to overcome the resistance of powerful internal enemies, often munitioned from without, but also that they lived in constant danger of attack from foreign States. No doubt Lenin and his colleagues were responsible, in the first seven years of the Revolution, for blunders, mistake, even crimes. It is nevertheless true that, in those years, they accomplished a remarkable work of renovation. They accomplished it, moreover, in such a fashion that, within ten years of the overthrow of the Czar, they were able to proceed to the full socialization of the productive system. In the last decade, the achievements have been immense. Unemployment has been abolished; illiteracy has been conquered; the growing productivity of the Soviet Union stands in startling contrast to the deliberate organization of scarcity in capitalist States. In the treatment of criminals, in the scientific handling of backward peoples, in the application of science to industry and agriculture, in the democratization of culture, in the conquest of racial prejudice, and the provision of opportunity to the individual—in the full sense the career opened to the talents—the Soviet Union stands today in the forefront of civilization. It is, of course, true that, judged by the standards of great Britain or the United States, its material levels of life are low; it has not rivalled in twenty years the unimpeded development of the most progressive capitalist states in a century. The answer, of course, is that the true comparison is with pre-revolutionary Russia; and there the gains, both material and spiritual, are immense. In wages, hours of labour, conditions of sanitation and safety, industrial security and educational opportunity, the comparison is at every point favourable to the new régime.

But it remains, after twenty years, definitely a dictatorship; and this has, naturally enough, caused grief and disappointment to those who care for freedom all over the world. Not only is it a dictatorship: but the ruthlessness with which it has suppressed those hostile to its authority has been sombrely seen in the grim tale of executions since the assassination of Kirov. In the classic sense of absolute liberalism freedom does not exist in the Soviet Union. There is no liberty to criticize the fundamentals of the régime. There is no liberty to found parties to oust the Communist leaders. A man cannot found a journal of opinion, or publish a book, or hold a meeting, to advocate views which, in the judgment of the dictatorship, would threaten the stability of the system. A citizen who sought to overthrow the philosophy of Marx, or to urge that Trotsky, and not Stalin, wears the true mantle of Lenin's tradition, would soon find himself on the way to exile or imprisonment. Art, the drama, music, the cinema, through all of these the dictatorship has sought to pour a stream of tendency, often with ludicrous, and sometimes with tragic, results.

To see the Soviet dictatorship in a proper perspective, certain things must be borne in mind. In the first place, with all its faults, it is wholly different in character from that of Mussolini or Hitler. Wide as are the differences in the rewards it confers, there is no evidence of the reappearance of a class that lives by owning; and it remains broadly true that differences in those rewards are related to the individual's contribution to the sum of social welfare. It is, moreover, the case that the purpose of the dictatorship is measurably and directly related to that welfare; its standard increasingly rises; it is built upon the principle of planned production for community consumption. It must, further, be remembered that the whole effort of the Soviet Union has been conducted throughout in an atmosphere of contingent war. If there has been little doubt of its internal stability since 1924, there has been constant reason, especially since 1933, to fear foreign attack; and the evidence goes only too plainly to show that its foreign enemies have counted upon, and even sought to stimulate, internal dissension and weakness, as the basis of that attack. And this must be set in the context of a people whose memories of the Civil Wars are vivid, who have been taught by their experience to find doctrinal differences arming themselves for ruthless conflict. They are aware that the basic principle of their social organization is, of its inherent nature, regarded by the rest of the world as a challenge; and they have been entitled by their experience to conclude that their strength and cohesion both measure with pretty rigorous accuracy the respect they are likely to achieve. They have suffered, as every new system suffers, from grave excess of bureaucratism and what Mr. and Mrs. Webb have happily termed the disease of orthodoxy. Their ruthlessness is, in part, an inheritance of an evil tradition, in part the almost inevitable technique of professional revolutionists who, unable by their principles to compromise, are accustomed to regard their lives as the stakes in the game. I know no evidence to suggest that Trotsky would have been less stern than Stalin in dealing with a challenge to his power; and the effective difference between his victims and those of the Czar is that the whole world regarded the latter as martyrs to a great cause. No such public opinion has been aroused by the trials of the Soviet prisoners as was aroused, for instance, by the execution of Sacco and Vanzetti, or the trial of Dimitrov.

To see the problem, once more, in its proper perspective one must think oneself back into a period like that of the Reformation. Then, as now, two great systems of social organization were struggling for mastery. Protestantism did not establish itself in twenty years. It took over a century and a quarter of bloody war for men to accept the compromise of live and let live. The Soviet experiment goes deeper than that of the Reformation in the changes of human behaviour it seeks to induce; it is not, I think, startling, therefore, that Stalin and his colleagues should not yet be prepared so to relax their authority as to permit its foundations to be called into question. They confront, of course, the danger that they, like all dictators, may be poisoned by the very volume of the power they possess so that they cling to it as absolute even when the need for its rigour has gone. I do not deny that danger. I do not deny, either, that the rulers of the Soviet Union have attracted their full share of fools and sycophants about them. On the other side there are some facts of significance to be borne in mind. The new Soviet Constitution is an immense step forward; one, certainly, that neither in form nor content would Fascist dictators dare to emulate. The second fact is the immense number of ordinary men and women, not themselves members of the dominant Communist Party, who share in the effective public administration of its life. The third fact is the enjoyment by the ordinary worker of a luxury of criticism about the details of his working life which is of immense significance to him, and largely inaccessible to his fellows under the capitalist system. Anyone who has been present at a meeting of a factory soviet, or read the wall newspapers in a shop or factory, knows well enough that the Soviet worker is a free man in a sense to which few English or American trade unionists can pretend. And he has at his disposal a freedom of access to his cultural heritage unrivalled under any capitalist system. In general, moreover, he has two great assets denied to his fellows elsewhere. The fear of unemployment has been removed from his life; and he has a confidence that, given international peace, he and, above all, his children face a future that consistently expands. He is still, no doubt, called upon for great sacrifices. But no one can visit the Soviet Union without the sense that its people feels itself to be the master of its own destiny in a way quite different from that realized by any other people.

On any showing, these are, I think, immense gains. They do not exclude the fact that the dictatorship throws heavy shadows still across the possible freedoms open to men. They do give reason to suppose that as men and women in the Soviet Union become accustomed to the ways of a new civilization, the sense of their secure establishment will necessarily mean the relaxation of the dictatorship. The vital things are, first, the removal of the fear of foreign intervention, with its corollary that Russian discontent is thereby encouraged to conspiratorial relationships; and, second, time enough for the mood to pass in which every opponent of the men in power seemed necessarily to be a revolutionary conspirator. If critics like Trotsky announce that the first condition of Russian salvation is the 'removal' of the present leaders, that is an incitement to reprisals which are bound to slow down the attainment of an atmosphere in which a full right of free criticism emerges. Granted all the shadows, the logic of the Russian system involves, in all normal circumstances, an ability to move forward to the revivification of principles of freedom.

That is not the case with the Fascist dictatorships. By their nature they involve the domination of the many in the interest of the few; by their nature, also, they involve military adventure which means the perpetual strains and stresses of nations organized for war. The purpose of Fascism is to prevent the relations of production coming into a natural harmony with the forces of production; for that prevention, and increasingly, the method of coercion is inescapable. Fascism has done nothing to deprive the holders of economic power of their privileges, save where these have been opponents of its policy. How should it do so, when its exponents have been the allies of, and financed by, the owners of economic power. It cannot permit the free expression of grievance; for, increasingly, this would be to admit the hollowness of its claims. It dare not permit freedom of association; were it to do so, its enemies would organize at once for battle against it. There is, in short, no way open to a Fascist dictatorship, as in logic there is to the rulers of the Soviet Union, to transform the processes of coercion into processes of consent. That ability was at the disposal of capitalism in its epoch of expansion. With the close of that epoch, it has either to fight democracy, or to submit to transformation by it. Fascism has chosen the first alternative; and over a wide area it has registered victories. But there is nothing of finality in their nature. There have been dark ages before in history; they mark the end of an economic system and the birth of a new. The Fascist enjoys today his uneasy hour of triumph. It is yet possible to discern in his vain glory the conscious fear of an impending doom.

IV

One last word is necessary. I do not mean by the prediction that Fascism contains the seeds of its own decay any assurance that its downfall will come quickly or that the victory will be an easy one. No one who looks at our world need doubt the power of reaction to fight vigorously for its privileges, its power, also, as it declines, to destroy no inconsiderable part of civilization. We shall have to pay heavily for that destruction; do not let us forget that it took Germany until the nineteenth century to recover from the Thirty Years' War. We may have to pay so heavily that, as in the Soviet Union, men may have to pass through an iron age before the reign of freedom is re-established.

Our business is to be prepared for the eventualities, so to organize ourselves that those to whom freedom matters are powerful enough to abridge as much as may be the period of difficulty. Amid all their perplexities, they have ground for hope. For they are entitled to the knowledge that the impulses of men to affirm their own essence rise superior to every effort at suppression; even the slave will dream that one day he may be free. They have the right to emphasize that, if liberty is stricken, the conquests of science over nature are inhibited at every turn. They can be confident, also, that men, however ignorant, will not finally endure the paradox of poverty and unemployment in a society that might be rich and secure. They will need, indeed, great qualities if they are to win, courage, above all, and the power to endure with resignation the bitterness of temporary defeat. They will require the self-control that gives rein to the heart only as it is guided by the mind. They will need philosophy as well as faith, daring not less than patience. It is the glory of freedom that it brings these qualities to those who serve it with fidelity. Before now, it has transformed a prison into an altar. Before now, it has brought the light of unconquerable hope into places that seemed utterly dark. We who fight the battle of freedom can maintain at least one certainty. We know that alone among the ends men seek it has the genius, where the need of its service is imperative, to give the quality of heroes to the common men who answer its call.

1937　　　　　　　　　　　HAROLD J. LASKI

CHAPTER I

INTRODUCTORY

I

I MEAN by liberty the absence of restraint upon the existence of those social conditions which, in modern civilization, are the necessary guarantees of individual happiness. I seek to inquire into the terms upon which it is attainable in the Western world, and, more especially, to find those rules of conduct to which political authority must conform if its subjects are, in a genuine sense, to be free.

Already, therefore, I am maintaining a thesis. I am arguing, first, that liberty is essentially an absence of restraint. It implies power to expand, the choice by the individual of his own way of life without imposed prohibitions from without. Men cannot, as Rousseau claimed, be forced into freedom. They do not, as Hegel insisted, find their liberty in obedience to the law. They are free when the rules under which they live leave them without a sense of frustration in realms they deem significant. They are unfree whenever the rules to which they have to conform compel them to conduct which they dislike and resent. I do not deny that there are types of conduct against which prohibitions are desirable: I ought, for instance, to be compelled, even against my wish, to educate my children. But I am arguing that any rule which demands from me something I would not otherwise give is a diminution of my freedom.

A second implication is important. My thesis involves the view that if in any state there is a body of men who possess unlimited political power, those over whom they rule can never be free. For the one assured result of historical investigation is the lesson that uncontrolled power is invariably poisonous to those who possess it. They are always tempted to impose their canon of good upon others, and, in the end, they asume that the good of the community depends upon the continuance of their power. Liberty always demands a limitation of political authority, and it is never attained unless the rulers of a state can, where necessary, be called to account. That is why Pericles insisted that the secret of liberty is courage.

By making liberty the absence of restraint, I make it, of course, a purely negative condition. I do not thereby mean to assume that a man will be the happier the more completely restraints are absent from the society to which he belongs. In a community like our own, the pressure of numbers and the diversity of desires make necessary both rules and compulsions. Each of these is a limitation upon freedom. Some of them are essential to happiness, but that does not make them for a moment less emphatically limitations. Our business is to secure such a balance between the liberty we need and the authority that is essential as to leave the average man with the clear sense that he has elbowroom for the continuous expression of his personality.

Nor must we confound liberty with certain other goods without which it has no meaning. There may be absence of restraint in the economic sphere, for example, in the sense that a man may be free to enter any vocation he may choose. Yet if he is deprived of security in employment he becomes the prey of a mental and physical servitude incompatible with the very essence of liberty. Nevertheless, economic security is not liberty, though it is a condition without which liberty is never effective. I do not mean that those

who can take their ease in Zion are thereby free men.
Once and for all, let us agree that property alone does
not make a man free. But those who know the normal
life of the poor, its perpetual fear of the morrow, its
haunting sense of impending disaster, its fitful search
for a beauty which perpetually eludes, will realize well
enough that, without economic security, liberty is not
worth having. Men may well be free and yet remain
unable to realize the purposes of freedom.

Again, we live in a big world, about which, at our
peril, we have to find our way. There can, under these
conditions, be no freedom that is worth while unless
the mind is trained to use its freedom. We cannot,
otherwise, make explicit our experience of life, and so
report the wants we build upon that experience to the
centre of political decision. The right of the modern
man to education became fundamental to his freedom
once the mastery of Nature by science transformed
the sources of power. Deprive a man of knowledge,
and the road to ever greater knowledge, and you will
make him, inevitably, the slave of those more fortunate
than himself. But deprivation of knowledge is not a
denial of liberty. It is a denial of the power to use
liberty for great ends. An ignorant man may be free
even in his ignorance. In our world he cannot employ
his freedom so as to give him assurance of happiness.
A compulsory training of the mind is still compulsion.
It is a sacrifice of some liberty to a greater freedom
when the compulsion ceases.

Two other preliminary remarks are important to the
thesis I am urging. Everyone knows the danger to
freedom which exists in any community where there
is either special privilege on the one hand or what is
termed the Tyranny of the majority on the other.
John Stuart Mill long ago pointed out that in the early
history of liberty it was normally and naturally conceived

as protection against the tyranny of the political rulers. The latter disposed of a power to which their subjects were compelled to conform; and it became vital in the interest of freedom to limit that power either by the recognition of special immunities or by the creation of constitutional guarantees. But even in the modern state the underlying substance of the argument may not be neglected. Power as such, when uncontrolled, is always the natural enemy of freedom. It prevents the exercise of those capacities which are released for activity by the absence of restraint. Wherever it is possessed in excess, it tilts the balance of social action in favour of its possessors. A franchise limited to the owners of property means legislation in the interests of that class. The exclusion of a race or creed from a share in citizenship is, invariably, their exclusion also from the benefits of social action. In any state, therefore, where liberty is to move to its appointed end, it is important that there should be equality.

Now equality is not the same thing as liberty. I do not, indeed, agree with Lord Acton's famous dictum that the 'passion for equality makes vain the hope of freedom'; [1] liberty and equality are not so much antithetic as complementary. Men might be broadly equal under a despotism, and yet unfree. But it is, I think, historically true that in the absence of certain equalities no freedom can ever hope for realization. The acute mind of Aristotle long ago saw that the craving for equality is one of the most profound roots of revolution. The reason is clear enough. The absence of equality means special privilege for some and not for others, of a special privilege which is not, so to say, in nature but in a deliberate contrivance of the social environment. Men like Harrington and Madison and Marx all insisted, and with truth, that whatever the forms of state, political

[1] Acton, *History of Freedom*, p. 57.

power will, in fact, belong to the owners of economic
power. We need not argue that our happiness depends
upon the possession of political power; we can argue
that exclusion from it is likely to mean exclusion from
that which largely determines the contours of happiness.
And it follows that the more equal are the social rights
of citizens, the more likely they are to be able to utilize
their freedom in realms worthy of exploration. Certainly
the history of the abolition of special privilege has been,
also, the history of the expansion of what in our
inheritance was open to the common man. The more
equality there is in a State, the more use, in general,
we can make of our freedom.

Here, perhaps, it is worth while for a moment to
dwell upon the meaning of equality. Nothing is easier
than to make it a notion utterly devoid of all common
sense.[1] It does not mean identity of treatment. The
ultimate fact of the variety of human nature, our
difference of both hereditary capacity and social nurture,
these are inescapable. To treat men so different as
Newton and Byron, Cromwell and Rousseau, in a
precisely similar way is patently absurd. But equality
does not mean identity of treatment. It is an insistence
that there is no difference inherent in nature between
the claims of men to happiness. It is therefore an
argument that society shall not construct barriers against
those claims which weigh more heavily upon some than
upon others. It shall not exclude men from the legal
profession because they are black or Wesleyans or freemasons. It shall not deny access to the Courts to men
of whose opinions society in general disapproves. The
idea of equality is obviously an idea of levelling. It is
an attempt to give each man as similar a chance as
possible to utilize what powers he may possess. It

[1] As Mr. Aldous Huxley, for instance, does with a quite unnecessary apparatus of scholarship in his *Proper Studies*, pp. 1–31.

means that he is to count in the framing of decisions
where these affect him, that whatever legal rights inhere
in any other man as a citizen, shall inhere in him also;
that where differences of treatment are meted out by
society to different persons, those differences shall be
capable of explanation in terms of the common good.
It means the recognition of urgent need in all—food,
for instance, and clothing, and shelter—before there
is special recognition of non-urgent claims in any.

Equality, so regarded, seems to me inescapably
connected with freedom. For equality, so regarded,
seems, in the first place, to mean the organization of
opportunities; and, in the second place, it means that
no man's opportunities are sacrificed, except on terms
of social principle, to the claims of another. Let me
illustrate by a simple example. On the view I am taking,
no child could be deprived of education that another
might receive it; but in a choice of men say for a post
in the Treasury, one might be preferred to another on
the ground of ability or character or training. The
idea of equality, in a word, is such an organization of
opportunity that no man's personality suffers frustration
to the private benefit of others. He is given his chance
that he may use his freedom to experiment with his
powers. He knows that in his effort to attain happiness
no barriers impede him differently from their incidence
upon others. He may not win his objective, but, at
least, he cannot claim that society has so weighted
the scale against him as to assure his defeat.

The second consideration I have noted will take us
further afield. It is often argued that a theory of liberty
which starts from the effort of the individual to attain
happiness must break down because it fails to remember
that society also has rights, and that these are necessarily
superior to those of its component parts. Any organization, it is said, is more than the units of which it is

composed. A nation-state like America or England is not merely a body of Englishmen or Americans, but something beyond them. It has a life and a reality, needs and purposes, which are not exhausted by the sum of the needs and purposes of its individual members. The liberty of each citizen is born of, and must be subordinated to, the liberty of that greater whole from which his whole meaning is derived. For the rights of each of us depend upon the protective rampart of social organization. It is because the State enforces our rights as obligations upon others that we have the opportunity to enjoy them. We are free, it is said, not for ourselves but for the society which gives us meaning. Where our interests conflict with the obviously greater interest of the society, we ourselves must give way.

It is, I think, true to say that an individual abstracted from society and regarded as entitled to freedom outside its environment is devoid of meaning. None of us is Crusoe or St. Simeon Stylites on his pillar. We are born to live our lives in London or New York, Paris or Berlin or Rome. Our liberty has to be realized in a welter of competing and co-operating interests which only achieve rational co-ordination by something not unlike a miracle. The need to give way to others, to accept, that is, restraint upon our right to unfettered activity is inherent in the nature of things. But the surrender we make is a surrender not for the sake of the society regarded as something other than its members, but exactly and precisely for men and women whose totality is conveniently summarized in a collective and abstract noun. I do not understand how England, for instance, can have an end or purpose different from, or opposed to, the end or purpose of its citizens. We strive to do our duty to England for the sake of Englishmen; a duty to England separate from them, and in which they did not share, is surely inconceivable.

Or, at least, would be inconceivable, were it not that perhaps the most influential theory of the state in our own time has been built upon it. What is termed the idealist theory of the State is broadly the argument that individual freedom means obedience to the law of the society to which I belong. My personality, it is said, is simply an expression of the organized whole to which I belong. When I say that I am seeking to realize myself, I mean in fact that I am seeking to be one with the order of which I am a part. I am not independent of, or isolated in, that order, but one with it and of it. As it realizes itself, so am I also realized. The greater and more powerful it becomes, the greater and more powerful do I become as a consequence. The more fully, therefore, I serve it, the more fully do I express myself. True liberty is thus so far from being an absence of restraint that it is essentially subordination to a system of rational purposes which receive their highest expression in the activity of the State. To be one with that activity may well then be regarded as the highest freedom a citizen can know.

In the whole history of political philosophy there is nothing more subtle than the skill with which the idealist school has turned the flank of the classic anti-thesis between liberty and authority. From the Greeks to Rousseau it was always conceived that a man's freedom is born of a limitation upon what his rulers may exact from him; since Rousseau, and, more particularly, since Hegel, it has been urged that con-formity to a code, and even compulsory obedience to it, is the very essence of freedom. So startling a paradox needs, at the least, explanation. Liberty, it argues, is not a mere negative thing like absence of restraint. It is rather a positive self-determination of the will which, in each of us, seeks the fulfilment of rational purpose as this lies behind, and gives unified meaning to, the diversified chaos of purposes in each of us. We desire freedom, that is to say, in order that we may be ourselves at our best. The right object of our wills, the thing which, did we know all the facts, we would truly desire, this is clearly that for which we would seek freedom. This is our real will, and the highest part of ourselves. This will, moreover, is the same in each member of society; for, at bottom, the real will is a common will which finds its highest embodiment in the State. In this view, therefore, the State is the highest part of ourselves. For it represents, in its will, what each of us would seek to be if the temporary, the immediate and the irrational, were stripped from the objects we desire. Its object is what alone we should aim at were we free to will only our permanent good. It is, so to say, the long and permanent end that, in the ultimate analysis, we come individually to will after private experience of wrong direction and erroneous desire. The more intimately, therefore, we make our will one with that of the State, the more completely are we free. The nature of the social bond makes service to its demands the very essence of freedom.

Before I seek to analyse this view, I would point out how simply this argument enables us to resolve the very difficult problem of social obligation. When I obey the State, I obey the best part of myself. The more fully I discover its purposes the more fully, also, there is revealed to me their identity with that at which, in the long view, I aim. So that when I obey it, I am, in fact, obeying myself; in a real sense its commands are my own. Its view is built upon the innumerable intelligences from the interplay of which social organization derives its ultimate form; obviously such a view is superior in its wisdom to the result my own petty knowledge can attain. My true liberty is, therefore, a kind of permanent tutelage to the State, a sacrifice of my limited purpose to its larger end upon the ground that, as this larger end is realized, so I, too, am given realization. I may, in fact, be most fully free when I am most suffused with the sense of compulsion.

To me, at least, this view contradicts all the major facts of experience. It seems to me to imply not only a paralysis of the will, but a denial of that uniqueness of individuality, that sense that each of us is ultimately different from his fellows, that is the ultimate fact of human experience. For as I encounter the State, it is for me a body of men issuing orders. Most of them, I can obey either with active good will or, at least, with indifference. But I may encounter some one order, a demand, for instance, for military service, a compulsion to abandon my religious faith, which seems to me in direct contradiction to the whole scheme of values I have found in life. How I can be the more free by subordinating my judgment of right to one which directly changes that judgment to its opposite, I cannot understand. If the individual is not to find the source of his decisions in the contact between the outer world and himself, in the experience, that is, which is the one unique thing that separates him from the rest of society, he ceases to have meaning as an individual in any sense that is creative. For the individual is real to himself not by reason of the contacts he shares with others, but because he reaches those contacts through a channel which he alone can know. His true self is the self that is isolated from his fellows and contributes the fruit of isolated meditation to the common good which, collectively, they seek to bring into being.

A true theory of liberty, I urge, is built upon a denial of each of the assumptions of idealism. My true self is not a selected system of rational purposes identical with those sought by every member of society. We cannot split up the wholeness of personality in this way. My true self is all that I am and do. It is the total impression produced by the bewildering variety of my acts, good and bad and indifferent. All of them go to the formation of my view of the universe; all of them are my expression of my striving to fulfil my personality. Each, while it is, is real, and each, as real, must give way only in terms of a judgment I make, not of one made for me by some other will, if I am to remain a purposive human being serving myself as an end. This attempt, in a word, at the extraction of a partial self from the whole of my being as alone truly myself not only denies that my experience is real, but, also, makes me merely an instrument to the purpose of others. Whatever that condition is, surely it cannot be recognized as freedom.

But we can go further than this. I see no reason to suppose that this assumed real will is identical in every member of society. The ultimate and inescapable fact in politics is the final variety of human wills. There is no continuum which makes all of them one. Experience suggests common objects of desire, but each will that wills these common objects is a different will in every sense, not purely metaphorical. We all have a will to international peace. But the unity these make is not in the will but in the fusion of separate wills to the attainment of a common purpose. And we must remember that in every society the objects of wills cannot, in some mystic fashion, be fused into a higher unity somehow compounded of them all. I see no meaning, for instance, in the statement that the antithetic purposes of Jesuits and Freemasons are somehow transcended in a higher purpose which presumes them both; that is to say that a Jesuit or a Freemason is most truly himself when he ceases to be himself, which, frankly, seems to me nonsense. A member of the Praesidium of the Third International, whose will aims supremely at the

overthrow of capitalism, is not somehow at one with
the will of the President of the British Federation of
Industries to whom all the purposes of the Third International are anathema. Both, doubtless, will the good;
but the point is that each wills the good as he sees
it, and each would regard the fulfilment of the other's
ideal of good as a definite destruction of his own.
There is, therefore, no single and common will in
society, unless we mean thereby the vague concept,
entirely useless for political philosophy, that men desire
the good. Each of us desires the good as he sees it;
and each of us sees a good derived from an individual
and separate experience into which no other person
can fully enter. Our connection with others is, at the
best, partial and interstitial. Our pooling of experiences
to make a common purpose somewhere is in no case
other than fragmentary. We remain ourselves even
when we join with others to attain some common
object of desire. The ultimate isolation of the individual
personality is the basis from which any adequate theory
of politics must start.

I reject, therefore, the idea of a real will, and, still
more, the idea that there is a common will in society.
It is a logical inference therefrom that I should reject
also the doctrine that all State-action is, at bottom,
the exercise of the real will of society. For, first of all,
I see no reason to suppose that social life is ultimately
the product of a single and rational mind organizing
its activities in terms of a logical process. To speak
of the 'mind of society' seems to me merely a metaphorical way of describing a course of action which
is made valid by translation into fact. There are no
governing principles in social life deliberately emerging
from the interplay of its myriad constituent parts.
Governing principles emerge; but they emerge through
the wills of individual minds. And the State is magnified

to excess when it is regarded as embodying a unified will. The State is a complex of rulers and subjects territorially organized and seeking, by the conference of power upon those rulers, effective co-ordination of social activities. They exercise the right to use force, if necessary, to that end. But no one, I think, can examine the course of history and say that the experience of any State indicates a permanent embodiment of the highest good we know in the purpose of the State. Our rulers, doubtless, aim at the good as they see it. Yet what they see as good may not be so recognizable to us, and may well provoke in us the sense that life would not be worth living if their view was to prevail. The unity of the State, in a word, is not inherently there. It is made by civic acceptance of what its rulers propose. It is not necessarily good because it is accepted; it is not necessarily right because it is proposed. Obedience ought always to be a function of the substance contained in the rules made by government; it is a permanent essay in the conditional mood.[1]

Here, of course, the idealist retorts that he is dealing not with the States of history, but with the State as such; he is concerned with the 'pure' instance and not with deviations from the ideal.[2] But it is with actual States that we have to deal in everyday life as we know it, with States the policy of which is directed by men who are human like ourselves. The policy they announce must, obviously, be subject to our scrutiny; and the result of our judgment is necessarily made out of an experience not identical with, even though it be similar to, theirs. I cannot believe that a theory fits the facts of history which assumes that this policy is going to be right, whatever it is; and that freedom will be found

[1] All this has been put in classic form by the late Professor Hobhouse in his *Metaphysical Theory of the State* (1918).
[2] Cf. Barker, *Political Thought from Herbert Spencer to Today* (1915), p. 80.

only in acceptance of it. I do not believe that the Huguenot of 1685 was made the more free by accepting, against his conscience, the Revocation; nor do I believe that Luther would have been more free had he accepted the decrees of Rome and abandoned his protest. Man is a one among many obstinately refusing reduction to unity. His separateness, his isolation, are indefeasible; indeed, they are so ultimate that they are the basis out of which his civic obligations are builded. He cannot abandon the consequences of his isolation which are, broadly speaking, that his experience is private and the will built out of that experience personal to himself. If he surrenders it to others, he surrenders his personality. If his will is set by the will of others, he ceases to be master of himself. I cannot believe that a man no longer master of himself is in any meaning sense free.

II

If we reject a view which, like that just considered, seeks to dissolve the reality of the individual into the society of which he is a part, what are we left with as the pattern within which a man seeks freedom? Let us try and draw a picture of the place of man in a community like our own. He finds himself involved in a complex of relationships out of which he must form such a pattern of conduct as will give him happiness. There are his family, his friends, the church to which he may belong, his voluntary association, trade union, or employers' association or whatever it may be, and there is the State. All of these, save the State, he may in greater or less degree avoid. A man may cut himself off from family or friends; he may refuse membership of a church or vocational body; he cannot refuse membership of the State. Somewhere or other, he encounters it as a body of persons issuing orders, and he is involved in the problem of deciding whether or no he will obey those orders. The point I want to make at the moment is this: every order issued is, in a final analysis, issued by a person or persons to another person or persons. When we say that, in such a complex or relationships as this, that a man is free, what do we mean? We know that if his church issues an order to him of which he disapproves, he can leave his church; so, too, with all other bodies save the State. The latter can, if he seeks evasion of its commands, use compulsion to secure obedience to its orders. It makes, we say, the law, and a member of the State is legally compelled to obey the law.

But he is not free, as I have argued, merely because he obeys the law. His freedom, in relation to the law, depends on the effect of any particular order upon his experience. He is seeking happiness; some order seems to him a wanton invasion of that happiness. He may be right or wrong in so thinking; the point of fact is that he has no alternative but to go by his own moral certainties. Now freedom exists in a State where a man knows that the decisions made by the ultimate authority do not invade his personality. The conditions of freedom are then those which assure the absence of such invasion. The citizen who asks for freedom is entitled to the conditions which, collectively, are the guarantees that he will be able to go on the road to his happiness, as he conceives it, unhindered. Neither conditions nor guarantees will ever be perfect; nor will they ever cover all upon which happiness depends. The State, for instance, may say that I may marry the woman I love; it cannot say that she will marry me if I so desire. The freedom it secures to me is the absence of a barrier in the way of marriage if I can win her consent.

From this angle, liberty may appropriately be resolved into a system of liberties. There are realms of conduct

within which, to be free, I must be permitted to act
as I please; to be denied self-expression there, is to be
denied freedom. What we need to know is, I suggest,
first what those realms of conduct are, and, second,
what my duty as a citizen is when I am, in any one of
them, prohibited from acting as I please. The difficulty
here, of course, it is impossible to exaggerate. It is
the problem of knowing when a man ought deliberately
to make up his mind to break the law or to refuse
obedience to it. In the idealist theory, this probem
does not arise; it is answered *a priori* by the definition
of freedom as obedience to the law. But because we
have rejected this view, we have to admit that there
will be occasional disobedience, at the least, and that
this may be justified. We have to discover the principles
of its justification.

Liberty, I have said, may be resolved into a system
of liberties; and from this angle it may be said that
it is the purpose of social organization to see to it
that this system is adequately safeguarded. How can
the State, which charges itself with the function of
supreme co-ordination, properly fulfil this task? How
can it guarantee to me such an environment to my
activity that I do not suffer frustration in my search
for happiness?

There have been many answers to this question, some
of them of the highest interest and importance. One
or two I wish to consider partly because of their significance in themselves, and partly because, from that
consideration, I wish to make the inference that no
merely mechanical arrangements will ever secure freedom
in permanence to the citizens of a State. While there
are certain constitutional forms which are, as I think,
essential to freedom, their mere presence as forms will
not, of themselves, suffice to make men free. I shall
seek, further, to draw the conclusion that, whatever

the forms of social organization, liberty is essentially an expression of an impalpable atmosphere among men. It is a sense that in the things we deem significant there is the opportunity of continuous initiative, knowledge that we can, so to speak, experiment with ourselves, think differently or act differently, from our neighbours without danger to our happiness being involved therein. We are not free, that is, unless we can form our plan of conduct to suit our own character without social penalties. Freedom is in an important degree a matter of law; but in a degree not less important it is a matter, also, of the *mores* of the society outside the sphere within which law can operate.

You will observe that I am still, from the angle of political organization, thinking of liberty as a safe-guard of the individual against those who rule him. I do so for the best of reasons. Whoever exerts power in a community is tempted to the abuse of power. Even in a democracy, we must have ways and means of protecting the minority against a majority which seeks to invade its freedom. Mankind has suffered much from the assumption that, once the people had become master in its own house, there was no limit to its power. You have only to remember the history of racial minorities like the negroes, of religious or national minorities like Jews and Czechs, to realize that democracy, of itself, is no guarantee of freedom. This raises the larger question of whether freedom in the modern State can ever be satisfactorily secured by internal sanctions, and whether, in fact, it is ever durably possible save in the terms of a strong and stable inter-national organization. For, clearly, we must not think of freedom as involving only an individual set over against the community; it involves also the freedom of groups, racial, ecclesiastical, vocational, set over against the community and the State; it involves also

c

the relation of States to on another, as, for instance, in the problem of annexation. No Englishman would think himself free if his domestic life were defined for him by another State; and no German but has had a bitter sense of unfreedom during the foreign occupation of the Rhineland. Our generation, at least, is unlikely to under-estimate the problem of what limits may be set to the demand for freedom by a national group.

III

Everyone who considers the relation of liberty to the institutions of a State will, I think, find it difficult to resist the conclusion that without democracy there cannot be liberty. That is not an over-popular thesis in our time. A reaction against democratic ideals is the fashion, and the dictatorships which proliferate over half Europe are earnest in maintaining their obsolescence. Yet consider, for a moment, what democracy implies. It involves a frame of government in which, first, men are given the chance of making the government under which they live, in which, also, the laws that government promulgates are binding equally upon all. I do not think the average man can be made happy merely by living in a democracy: I do not see how he can avoid a sense of continuous frustration unless he does. For if he does not share in making the government, if he cannot, where his fellows so choose, be himself made one of the rulers of the State, he is excluded from that which secures him the certainty that his experience counts. To read the history of England before the enfranchisement of the wage-earner is to realize that however small is the value of the franchise it still assures the attention of government to grievance. The right, therefore, to the franchise is essential to liberty; and a citizen excluded from it is unfree. Unfree for the simple reason that

the rulers of the State will not regard his will as entitled
to consideration in the making of policy. They will
do things for him, but not those things he himself
regards as urgent; as Parliament a hundred years ago
met the grim problem of urban want by building more
churches to the glory of the Lord. Whatever is to be
said against the democratic form of State, it seems to
me unquestionable that it has forced the needs of
humble men on the attention of government in a way
impossible under any other form.

To be free, I argue, a people must be able to choose
its rulers at stated intervals simply because there is
no other way in which their wants, as they experience
those wants, will receive attention. It is fundamental
to the conference of power that it should never be
permanent. If it is so, it ceases to give attention to
the purposes for which it is conferred and thinks only
of the well-being of those who can exercise it. That
has been, notably, the history of monarchy and aristocracy, and in general, of the practice of colonial
dominion. Power that is unaccountable makes instruments of men who should be ends in themselves.
Responsible government in a democracy lives always
in the shadow of coming defeat; and this makes it eager
to satisfy those with whose destinies it is charged.

That is a general principle which, stated as baldly
as this, does not adequately illustrate the substance
it implies. The history of the struggle for popular
freedom has given us knowledge of certain rules in the
organization of a State the presence of which is fundamental to freedom. It can, I think, be shown that no
citizen is secure in liberty unless certain rights are
guaranteed to him, rights which the government of
the State cannot hope to overthrow; and unless, to
secure the maintenance of those rights, there is a separation of the judicial from the executive power.

Let me take the second of these principles first. The citizens of a State choose men to make the laws under which they are to live. It is urgent that they should be binding upon all without fear or favour; that I, for instance, should be able to live secure in the knowledge that they will not apply to me differently from their incidence upon others. Clearly enough, in the modern State, the application of law to life demands a vast body of civil servants to administer it. Not the least important problem of our time is that which arises when the legality of their administration is in question. In Anglo-Saxon communities it has been regarded as elementary that the interpretation of law should be entrusted to an independent body of officials—the judges—who can arbitrate impartially between government and citizens. That view I take to be of the first importance to freedom; and its acceptance involves considerations which we must examine in some detail.

The business of a judiciary, broadly speaking, is the impartial interpretation of the law as between government and citizen, or between classes of citizens who dispute with one another. The government, for instance, charges a man with treason; obviously he is deprived of something essential to his freedom if the law is strained so as to make of treason something it in fact is not, in order to cover the acts which the government seeks to have accepted as treason. Here, obviously, the judge must be assured that his independence may be maintained with safety to himself. He must not suffer in his person or position because of the view he takes. It must not be within the power either of the government or other persons to deprive him of his authority because, as best he may, he applies the law. This, as I think, makes it essential that all judicial appointments should be held during good behaviour. There may be an age-limit of service, of course; but, this apart, nothing should permit the removal of a judge from the bench except corruption of physical unfitness. I do not, therefore, believe that a judicial system founded upon popular election is a satisfactory way of choosing judges, the more so if submission to re-election is involved; and the system, abandoned in England in 1701, of making judicial appointment dependent upon the pleasure of government is equally indefensible. Once a man has been appointed to judicial office nothing must stand in the way of his complete independence of mind. Election, re-election, a power in the government to dismiss, are all of them incompatible with the function the judge is to perform. They will not, as a general rule, either give us the men we want, or enable us to keep them when we have found them.

But we must, I think, go further than this. Judicial independence is not merely a matter of mechanical technique; it is also psychological in character. The judge whose promotion is dependent upon the will of the executive, even more, the judge who may look to a political career as a source of future distinction, neither of these is adequately protected in that independence of mind which is the pivot of his function. No less a person than Mr. Chief Justice Taft has told us that he appointed a predecessor to that eminent position at least partly because he approved of one of his decisions.[1] No one could, I think, have confidence in the Bench if it were known that decisions pleasing to a given political party might lead either to promotion or to choice as either a presidential candidate or as Lord Chancellor. It seems to me, therefore, that we must so organize the method of judicial promotion as to prevent the executive from choosing men of its

[1] W. H. Taft, *Our Supreme Magistrate and His Powers* (1921), pp. 102–3.

own outlook, and, further, see to it that appointment
to the Bench is definitely taken as the end of a political
career. These are problems of detailed technique into
which I cannot now enter;[1] here I am only concerned
to point out that the problem of independence which
they raise is one that it is necessary to meet with
frankness.

But the judge's authority as a safeguard of our
freedom is in the modern State threatened in another
way. Modern legislation is so huge both in volume
and extent that the average assembly has neither time
nor energy to scrutinize its details. The modern habit
is, therefore, to pass Acts which confer a general power,
and to leave the filling in of details to the discretion of
the department concerned. To this, I think, no one
can really take exception. The State must do its work;
and it must develop the agencies necessary to that end.
But I think we have grave reason for fear when the
growth of this delegated legislative authority is accom-
panied with, or followed by, the conference of powers
upon government departments themselves to determine
the question of whether the powers they take are legal
or not. I regard the growth of delegated legislation as
both necessary and desirable; but if it is not gravely
to impair our freedom, it should, I think, be developed
only under the amplest safeguards.

Decisions, for instance, like that on the *Ju Toy* case [2]
in the United States, and in *Arlidge* v. *Local Government
Board* [3] in England, are clearly a real menace to the
liberty of the subject. They suggest a type of executive
justice for which the methods of the Star Chamber are
the nearest analogy. No body of civil servants, however

[1] See my detailed discussion of the point in 34 Michigan Law
Review, p. 529.
[2] 189 U.S. 253.
[3] (1915) A.C. 120.

liberal-minded they may be, ought to be free both to make the law and to devise the procedure by which its legality may be tested; and that, be it remembered, without a power of appeal from their decision. It may be taken for granted that the modern State needs an administrative law; in matters, for instance, like rate-fixing in public utilities, in workmen's compensation cases, in matters concerning public health, the views of a body of experts in a public department are generally at least as valid as that of the judicial body. But one wants to be certain that in arriving at his decision the expert has been compelled to take account of all the relevant evidence; that the parties to his decision have had their day in court. This seems to me to involve the organization of a procedure for all administrative tribunals which takes account of the lessons we have learned both from the procedure of ordinary courts and from the history of the law of evidence; and it involves an appeal from administrative tribunals to the ordinary courts on all questions where denial of proper procedure is held to involve a denial of proper considera-tion. Something of this, if I understand the matter aright, has been granted to the American citizen by the Supreme Court in *McCall &c.* v. *New York* [1]; and I should feel happier about the future of administrative law if I were certain that the principles of that decision applied to all govermental activities of the kind.

Another safeguard is not less essential. We agree, for the most part, in ordinary legal matters that the opinion of a single judge, even when reinforced by the verdict of a jury, ought not to be final in either criminal or civil cases. I should like to see that agreement extended to the sphere of administrative law. Where, that is to say, a departmental tribunal has rendered its decision I should like an appeal to lie to a higher

[1] 38 Sup. Ct. Rep. 122.

administrative tribunal composed not only of officials, but, also, of laymen of experience in the matters involved who could be trusted to bring an independent mind to the settlement of the matter in dispute. English experience of tribunals like the civil service division of the Industrial Court, and the Commissioners of Income Tax, convinces me that the common sense of a good lay mind is, in this realm, an immense safeguard against departmental error. And we must remember that, however great be the good will of the public services, what, to them, may seem a simple matter of administrative routine, may be to the citizens involved a denial of the very substance of freedom. Certainly a case like *ex parte O'Brien* [1] makes one see how real would be the threat to public liberty if departmental legislation grew without proper judicial scrutiny at every stage of its development.

The problem, however, does not merely end here. There are two other sides of administrative action in which the uncontrolled power of the State is an implicit threat to civic freedom. Of the first, I would say here only a word, since I have treated it fully elsewhere. [2] The modern State is a sovereign State and, as such, there are realms of its conduct where wrong on its part cannot imply the invocation by the citizen of penalty. The right to sue the State in tort seems to me quite fundamental to freedom. The modern State is in essence a public service corporation. Like any other body, it acts through servants who take decisions in its name. I can see no reason in the world why, like any other body serving the public, it should not be responsible for the torts of its agents. If I am run over by the negligent driver of a railway truck, I can secure damages; I do not see why I am not equally entitled

[1] (1923) 2 K.B. 61.
[2] Cf. my *Grammar of Politics*, pp. 541 ff.

to damages if the truck is the property of, and is driven for, the Postmaster-General of His Majesty.[1]

But, still in the context of administration, the needs of liberty go yet further. There has accreted today about the departments of State a type of discretionary power which seems to me full of danger unless it is exercised under proper safeguards. Examples of it are the power of the Postmaster-General in the United States over the mails and of the Home Secretary in England over requests from aliens for naturalization. Let me deal with the latter authority since I am best acquainted with its character. An alien applies to the Home Secretary for naturalization. He answers innumerable questions, and presents certificates of good character from citizens who testify on oath to his standing. He has resided in the country for at least five years and he will not, of course, normally venture to apply unless his record is adequate. A request is published in the press for any information about him and, after a due interval, the Home Secretary makes a decision about his case. He has, of course, pursued his own inquiries, and he has, presumably, received information about the applicant upon which his action is based. Now the point that disturbs me is the fact that where a certificate of naturalization is refused, the grounds for rejection are never, even privately to the applicant, made known. He is refused privileges which may be vital to him and his family in the background of accusations which may, doubtless, be true, but may also be completely without foundation and capable, were opportunity afforded, of being immediately and decisively refuted. And so great is the discretionary power of the Minister that he may even substitute his own will for that of the legislature: the Act, for instance, demands a five-year period of residence. The late Home

[1] Cf. my *Grammar of Politics*, pp. 541 ff.

Secretary, Lord Brentford, announced that while he
was in office he would grant no certificate unless the
applicant had resided in England continuously for a
period of thirteen years. It seems to me that this power
to deny admission to citizenship, as it is exercised,
is a complete denial of natural justice. No person
ought to be condemned by accusations he is not given
the opportunity to refute. Anyone who wishes to give
testimony in a case of this kind ought surely to prove
his *bona fides* by submitting to cross-examination by
the applicant or his representative. I should like, therefore, to see the possibility of an appeal from the decision
of the Home Secretary to a judge in chambers where
the latter would, on a case stated by the Department,
hear such evidence as the applicant chose to bring for
its refutation and then only make a final decision.
Anything less than this seems to me a wanton abuse
of freedom; and, *mutatis mutandis*, this type of safeguard seems to me urgent wherever a Minister is given
a discretionary power which affects the liberty of the
subject.

I accept, therefore, the traditional notion that the
separation of the judicial from the executive power,
the right of the former to determine the legality of
executive decision, is the basis of freedom. I do not,
however, believe that the separation of the executive
from the legislature is either necessary or desirable.
The origin of the idea, as you know, is in the historic
misinterpretation of the British Constitution by Montes-
quieu[1]; and this, in its turn, was due to his misapplication
of certain classic dicta of Locke.[2] The fact is that a
separation in this realm results in a complete and
undesirable erosion of responsibility. The British
system, in which the executive, as a committee of the

---

[1] *Esprit des Lois*, Bk. XI, Chap. VI.
[2] Second Treatise, Sec. 12.

legislature, formulates its plans for acceptance or rejection, has, I think, the clear advantage of showing the electorate exactly where responsibility for action must lie. Where mistakes are made, where there is corruption, or dishonesty, or abuse, it can be brought home forthwith to its authors. In the American system, that is not the case. The President is neither the master nor the servant of the legislature. The latter can make its own schemes; where its views, more, where its party complexion, are different from his, there is a constant tendency to paralysis of administration. Each can blame the other for failure. No clear policy emerges upon which the electorate can form a straightforward judgment. Independence makes for antagonism and antagonism, in its turn, makes for confusion. Such a separation means, almost invariably, the construction of a separate quasi-executive in the legislature, which has an interest of its own distinct from, and often hostile to, that of the President.[1] I can see no necessary safeguard of liberty in this. On the contrary, the British system, where the executive may be at any moment destroyed by the legislature as a penalty for error or wrong, where, also, there lies always the prospect of an immediate and direct appeal to the people as the ultimate and only arbiter of difference, seems to me far more satisfactory.

IV

Another institutional mechanism for the safeguarding of freedom is that of a Bill of Rights. Certain principles, freedom of speech, protection from arbitrary arrest, and the like, are regarded as especially sacred. They are enshrined in a document which cannot, constitutionally, be invaded either by the legislature or the executive, save by a special procedure to which access

[1] Cf. my paper on American Federalism in the volume entitled *The Dangers of Obedience* (1930).

is difficult. The first Amendment to the American Constitution, for example, lays it down that Congress shall pass no law abridging freedom of speech; and any Act of Congress which touches upon the matter can be challenged for unconstitutionality before the Supreme Court. The Amendment, moreover, cannot be attacked save by the usual process of constitutional change in America; and that means that, except in the event of an American Revolution, it is unlikely ever to be directly attacked at all.

My own years of residence in the United States have convinced me that there is a real value in Bills of Rights which it is both easy, and mistaken, to under-estimate. Granted that the people are educated to the appreciation of their purpose, they serve to draw attention, as attention needs to be drawn, to the fact that vigilance is essential in the realm of what Cromwell called fundamentals. Bills of Rights are, quite undoubtedly, a check upon possible excess in the government of the day. They warn us that certain popular powers have had to be fought for, and may have to be fought for again. The solemnity they embody serves to set the people on their guard. It acts as a rallying-point in the state for all who care deeply for the ideals of freedom. I believe, for instance, that the existence of the First Amendment has drawn innumerable American citizens to defend freedom of speech who have no atom of sympathy with the purposes for which it is used. A Bill of Rights, so to say, canonizes the safeguards of freedom; and, thereby, it persuades men to worship at the altar who might not otherwise note its existence.

All this, I think, is true; but it does not for a moment imply that a Bill of Rights is an automatic guarantee of liberty. For the relationship of legislation to its substance has to be measured by the judiciary. Its members, after all, are human beings, likely, as the rest of us, to be swept off their feet by gusts of popular passion. The first Amendment to the American Constitution guarantees freedom of speech and peaceable assembly; the fourth Amendment legally secures to the citizen that his house shall not be searched except upon a warrant of probable cause; the eighth Amendment legally secures him against excessive bail. Yet you will remember how, in one hysterical week in 1919, the action of the executive power rendered all these amendments worthless[1]; and you will not forget that the fifteenth Amendment, which sought political freedom for the coloured citizens of the South, has never been effectively applied either by the executive or by the Courts.

The fact is that any Bill of Rights depends for its efficacy on the determination of the people that it shall be maintained. It is just as strong, and no more, as the popular will to freedom. No one now doubts that the Espionage Acts were strained so as to destroy almost all that the first Amendment was intended to cover; that most of the charges preferred under it were, on their face, ludicrous. Yet you will remember that, in *Abrams* v. *United States*,[2] two judges stood alone in their insistence that the first Amendment really meant something; the judgment of the others was caught in the meshes of war hysteria. No principle is better established than the right of the citizen, under proper circumstances, to a writ of *habeas corpus;* that is, perhaps, the ark of the covenant in the Anglo-American conception of freedom. But who can ever forget the noble and pathetic words of Chief Justice Taney, in *ex parte Merryman*,[3] where he insists that the applicant is entitled to the writ and that, in view

[1] Cf. Louis Post, *The Deportations Delirium* (1921).
[2] 250 U.S. 616.
[3] See Taney's *Report.*

of President Lincoln's suspension of it—a suspension
entirely illegal in character—he could not secure to
Mr. Merryman his due rights? And let us remember,
also, that even where the judge is prepared to do his
duty, he cannot, in a period of excitement, count upon
public opinion. Nothing is clearer than the fact that
those who hanged Mr. Gordon during the Jamaica
riots were guilty of murder. The opinion of Chief
Justice Cockburn could not have made the issue more
clear; it is a landmark in the judicial history of freedom.
Yet the jury at once, in its despite, acquitted the accused.
There have been, further, many occasions when breaches
of fundamental principles of freedom, breaches which,
on any showing, have been quite indefensible, have been
followed at once by Acts of Indemnity. I know only
of one case in England in the last hundred years in
which such an Act has been refused. Yet it is, I think,
obvious that unless such breaches are definitely and
deliberately punished, they will always occur on critical
occasions. At such times, it is impossible to trust those
who are charged with the exercise of power; and only
the knowledge that swift and certain punishment will
follow its abuse will make our rulers attentive to the
needs of freedom.

I speak the language of severity; and I am anxious
that you should not think that the language of severity
is that of the extremist. I invite you, as the proof of
what I say, to read, in the light of cold reason a decade
after the close of the war, the history of the tribunals
in England which were charged with examining con-
scientious objectors to military service and on the military
authorities to whom some of those objectors were
handed over.[1] No one can go through the record without the sense that some of the tribunals deliberately
evaded the purposes of the exemption clause; and it

[1] J. W. Graham, *Conscription and Conscience* (1922), Chap. III.

is clear that in the administration of punishment for
refusal to obey orders, there was wanton cruelty, a
deliberate pleasure in the infliction of pain, for which
no words can be too strong. Nor is that all. The
record shows occasions when Ministers of the Crown,
when responding to questions in the House of Commons,
used evasions of a kind which showed a complete contempt for truth;[1] and they were supported in their
attitude by the majority of the members there. I note,
also, at least one occasion when a number of conscien-
tious objectors were taken from England to France
for the purpose of execution by the military authorities;
and it was only the accident that Professor Gilbert
Murray was able to appeal on their behalf to the Prime
Minister, which prevented the sentence from being
carried out.[2] These are worse than the methods of the
Inquisition; for, at least, the members of that tribunal
believed that they were rescuing their victims from
eternal damnation. Those of whom I speak had no
excuse save ignorant prejudice and the blindness of
passion.

You will see, therefore, why I cannot believe that
constitutional expedients alone, however substantial,
will prevent the invasion of liberty. They will work
just so long as people are determined they shall work,
and no longer. They are valuable because, since they
have been consecrated by tradition, their invasion tends
to awaken, at least in some of us, a prejudice to which
we have become habituated. But to keep them active
and alive, requires a deliberate and purposive effort it
is by no means easy to make when the result of doing
so conflicts with some other object keenly desired.
That is, I think, capable of a simple demonstration.

[1] J. W, Graham, *Conscription and Conscience* (1922), Chap. III,
p. 209.
  [2] *Ibid.*

No class of men is so carefully trained as the judiciary to the habit of a balanced mind. Yet if you examine the observations of judges in cases where their passions are deeply involved you will note how great is the effort they have to make to show tolerance to antagonistic views. Nor do they always succeed. In most of the classic English blasphemy cases, for example, the judge has too often been, either consciously or unconsciously, an additional counsel for the prosecution.[1] In many of the American Espionage Acts cases what chiefly emerges from the summing up of the judge is a desire, at all costs, to see that the prisoner does not secure an acquittal.[2]   Recent injunction cases in America show a desire, no doubt unconscious, on the part of the Court, to lend aid and countenance to a social philosophy of which it happens to approve.

I conclude, therefore, that in general we shall not allow, as a society, the mechanisms of the state to serve the cause of freedom unless we approve the objects at which freedom aims.   In a time of crisis, particularly, when the things we hold most dear are threatened, we shall find the desire to throw overboard the habits of tolerance almost irresistible. For those habits are not in Nature, which teaches us that opinions we deem evil are fraught with death. They come from our social heritage, and are part of a process the value of which we must relearn continuously if we are to preserve it. That is the meaning of the famous maxim that eternal vigilance is the price of liberty. It is why, also, it becomes necessary in each age to restate the case for freedom, if it is to be maintained.

[1] See, for example, Wickwar's *Freedom of the Press* for an account of judicial *mores* in the early nineteenth century; and H. T. Buckle's pamphlet on the Pooley case for similar conduct thirty years later.

[2] Z. C. Chafee's classic discussion in *Freedom of Speech* is the best account of this unhappy period.

V

There is one other general part of this political aspect of liberty that I wish to consider before I turn to a different portion of my theme. I have argued that resistance to the encroachments of power is essential to freedom because it is the habit of power continuously, if it can, to enlarge the boundaries of its authority. Is there any specific rule by which men can be trained to such resistance? Is there, that is, a way in which the average citizen of the modern state can be persuaded that it is in his interest to be viligant against those who would invade his rights? Can it, further, be shown that such a temper in the citizen is likely, as it grows, to confer benefit upon the community as a whole?

Broadly speaking, I think the answer to these questions is in the affirmative. I hazard the generalization that the more widespread the distribution of power in the state, the more decentralized its character, the more likely men are to be zealous for freedom. That is, of course, a large statement to make. It is the thesis that, in terms of historic experience, good government is always, in the end, both less valuable and less efficient than self-government. I mean that, in general, rules imposed upon a society from above for its benefit are less effective to the end that they seek than rules which have grown naturally from below. I believe that to be true both of the individual and the group in society. Its full realization is, of course, an impossibility since it would make the uniformities we need in social life unattainable. But the greater the degree in which we can realize it, the better for the community to which we belong.

I do not mean to imply that there is any rigid principle which enables us to mark off the lines of demarcation between what is individual and what is social, between what belongs to the group and what belongs to the state, between the sphere of central, and the sphere of local government. The only possible approach to that problem is a pragmatic one, as anyone can see who tries to make common sense out of John Stuart Mill's famous attempt, with its list of exceptions[1] by which he reduced it to something like absurdity. Most of us, I think, could draw up lists of governmental subjects in which central and local topics could be demarcated without undue disagreement. We should fairly universally say that foreign policy and defence, fiscal technique and commercial regulation were naturally within the sphere of the central, as public libraries, baths and wash-houses and playing fields were within the sphere of the local, authority. We should agree that crime is a matter for the state, and sin a matter for the churches. We should admit that there must be uniform regulations for marriage and divorce, but that individuals only could make up their minds when, within the regulations, either to marry or divorce.

This, I think, is pretty straightforward. The points I wish to emphasize are different. They are, first, that in the making of public decisions, it is desirable that as many persons as possible who are affected by the result should share in reaching it; and, secondly, that whenever the decision to make some rule of conduct a matter of governmental regulation arouses widespread and ardent dissent, the probability is that the case against the decision is stronger than the case in its favour. Let us take each of these points separately.

My first point I may perhaps best make by the statement that all creative authority is essentially federal in character. The purpose for which authority is exercised is the maximum satisfaction of desire. To achieve that

[1] Thereby laying himself open to FitzJames Stephen's crushing attack.

end, it is in the long run vital to take account of the wills of those who will be affected by the decision. For, otherwise, their desires are unexplored, and there is substituted for the full experience that should be available, the partial experience, perhaps suffused with a sinister interest, which is able to influence the legal source of decision. Maximum satisfaction, in other words, is a function of maximum consultation; and the greater the degree in which the citizen shares in making the rules under which he lives, the more likely is his allegiance to those rules to be free and unfettered. Nor is this all. The process of being consulted gives him a sense of being significant in the State. It makes him feel that he is more than the mere recipient of orders. He realizes that the State exists for his ends and not for its own. He comes to see that his needs will be met only as he contributes his instructed judgment to the experience out of which decisions are compounded. He gains the expectation of being consulted, the sense that he must form an opinion on public affairs. He learns to dislike orders which are issued without regard being paid to his will. He comes to have a sense of frustration when decisions are made arbitrarily, and without an attempt to build them from the consent of those affected. He learns vigilance about the ways of power. Those who are trained to that vigilance become the conscious guardians of liberty.

For they will protest against what they regard as the invasion of their rights, and tribute will have to be paid to their protest. In any community, fortunately for ourselves, power is always upon the defensive; and when men are vigilant to expose its encroachments it is urgent to seek their good opinion. Those active-minded enough to fight for their rights will, doubtless, be always in a minority; but they prick the indifferent multitude into thought and they thus act as the gadflies of liberty. The handful of American lawyers who protested against the methods of the Department of Justice in 1920 forced its officials to a change of their ways. The little group of men who, in season and out of season, have protested that the white man's burden ought not, in justice, to be borne by the black, have the Mandates system of the League of Nations to their credit: what E. D. Morel did for the Congo, what H. W. Nevinson did for Portuguese Angola, these are lessons in the service of citizenship to liberty. And it is the peculiar value of this habit of mind that it grows by what it feeds on. To accustom the average man to regard himself as a person who must be consulted is, in the long run, to assure him, through consultation, of satisfaction. For the holders of power are always desirous of finding the convenient routine; and if they are driven by pressure to give the people freedom, they will discover that this is the object they have set before themselves.

Into the institutional pattern which such a federalization of authority requires I cannot here enter.[1] It must suffice to say that it makes totally inadequate the traditional forms even of the democratic State. For the notion that, when the citizen has chosen his representatives for Parliament or his local authority, he can sit back in the comfortable knowledge that his wants are known, his interests safeguarded, has not one jot of evidence to support it. We need, of a certainty, a much more complex scheme. We have not only to provide for more adequate relationships between Parliament and the administrative process; we have also to integrate the latter with the public it serves on a much ampler scale than any we have hitherto imagined. I have elsewhere tried to show how vital in this context is the device of the advisory committee. Its value both

[1] Cf. my *Grammar of Politics*, Chap. VII.

as a check upon bureaucracy, and as a means of making decision genuinely representative in character, becomes the more clear the wider our experience of its functioning.

But even this is not enough. There will never be liberty in any State where there is an excessive concentration of power at the centre. The need for a wide conference of authority away from that centre becomes more obvious with the growth of our experience. If the decisions to be made are to embody the needs of those affected by them, the latter must have major responsibility for their making. All of our problems are not central problems; and to leave to the central government the decision of questions which affect only a portion of the community is to destroy in that portion the sense of responsibility and the habit of inventivness. The inhabitants of any given area have a consciousness of common purposes, a sense of the needs of their neighbourhood, which only they can fully know. They find that the power to satisfy them of themselves gives to them a quality of vigour far greater in the happiness it produces than would be the case if satisfaction were always provided by, or controlled from, without. For administration from without always lacks the vitalizing ability to be responsive to local opinion; it misses shades and expressions of thought and want which are urgent to successful government. It lacks the genius of place. It does not elicit creative support from those over whom it rules. It makes for mechanical uniformity, an effort to apply similar rules to unsimilar things. It is too distant from the thing to be done to awaken interest from those concerned in the process of doing it. Centralized government in local matters may be more efficient than a decentralized system; but that superior efficiency will never, as Mill long ago pointed out, compensate for an inferior interest in the result.

I believe, therefore, that, with all its difficulties and dangers, the area of local government should be as little circumscribed as possible. The German system, of laying down what a local authority may not do, and leaving it free to experiment outside that realm of prohibition, seems to me superior both in principle and result to its Anglo-American antithesis. Thereby we gain not only the knowledge which comes from varied social experiment, but the freedom born of citizenship trained in the widest degree to think for itself and to solve its own problems. Most imposed solutions of a uniform character only succeed where their material is genuinely uniform. That is rarely the case in these matters. And even the impatient reformer ought sometimes to think whether, say, forcing a child-labour law on Georgia by federal amendment will lead to a genuine and whole-hearted application of its terms; whether, in fact, it will not persuade to hatred of the law, even contempt for the law, by encouraging evasion of it. Successful legisation is almost always legislation for which the minds of men are anxious; the channels of assent to it can rarely be dug too deep.

All, moreover, that I am saying of territorial locality, seems to me to apply, with no less emphasis, to what may be termed functional areas also. Everyone acquainted with the history of churches realizes the necessity of leaving them free to develop their own internal life. On matters like ecclesiastical government, dogma, ceremonial, interference by the State is almost invariably disastrous in its results. What is true of churches is true also, *mutatis mutandis*, of other associations. Bodies like the legal and medical professions are much better able to direct their own internal life than to have it directed for them by the State. It is necessary, of course, to prevent them from developing into monopolies; and to that end it is essential to devise a framework of principle within which they must work, to retain, also, the right to its revision from without from time to time. But that said, few would, I think, deny that what we call professional standards, the jealousy for the honour of the profession, the sense of *esprit de corps*, the realization that its members owe to the community something more than the qualities for which payment can be exacted, these things are born of the large degree of freedom to define their own life the professions enjoy.

It is, I think, important to extend that notion of self-government beyond the professions. We ought to learn to think of industries like cotton and coal as entities not less real than Lancashire or New York, as capable, therefore, of being organized for the purpose of government. Most of the plans as current today for national economic councils are not, in my judgment, of great value; the satisfactory weighting of the different elements is really insoluble, and any problem that concerns industry as a whole seems to me at once civic in its nature and, therefore, the proper province of the legislative assembly of the State.[1] But these considerations do not apply to industries taken individually, or linked together at special points of intimate contact. It does not seem to me inconceivable that we should create a Parliament for the mining industry, in which capital, management, labour and the consumer should each have their due representation, and to which should be confided the determination of industrial standards on the model of professional self-government. I should give to this Parliament a power of delegate legislation which would enable it to frame rules of conduct binding upon all the members of the industry. Thus, while Georgia might refuse to pass a child-labour law, a particular industry in Georgia might

[1] Cf. my *Grammar of Politics*, p. 82 f.

refuse to allow its members to engage child labour in field or factory. There might be developed in this way a body of industrial legislation and jurisprudence growing naturally out of the experience of those who participate in the operation of the industry, and imposed with a real sense of freedom because it has been developed from within and is not the outcome of an external control. The help this system would give to the creative-minded employer, on the one hand, and the adventurous trade-union, on the other, needs no emphasis from me. Something of what it might effect, if planned in a wholesale way, the experiments of the Amalgamated Clothing Workers and the Baltimore and Ohio Railroad have amply demonstrated. They show clearly, I venture to suggest, that an authority born of consent is always definitely superior to an authority born of coercion. And the reason is the simple but vital one that creative energy is liberated only in the atmosphere of freedom.

VI

In all that I have so far said there is implied a theory of the nature of law upon which, perhaps, I ought to say a word. The view I am taking suggests that law is not simply a body of commands justifiable by virtue of their origin. Laws are rules seeking to satisfy human desires. They are the more certain of acceptance the more fully they seek to inquire what desires it is urgent to satisfy, and the best way of inquiry is to associate men with each stage of the process of law-making. For men, in fact, will not obey law which goes counter to what they regard as fundamental. Their notion of what is fundamental may be wrong, or unwise, or limited ; but it is their notion, and they do not feel free unless they can act by their own moral certainties. It is useless to tell them that an assumption on their part that they are entitled to forgo obedience will result in anarchy. Every generation contains examples of men who, in the context of ultimate experience, deliberately decide that an anarchy in which they seek to maintain some principle is preferable to an order in which that principle must be surrendered. The South in 1861, Ulster in 1914, the Communist in the context of a capitalist society, these are but variations on the great theme of Luther's classic *Ich kann nicht anders*. They illustrate the inescapable truth that law must make its way to acceptance through the channel of consenting minds.

Let me put this in a different way. Law is not merely a command; it is also an appeal. It is a search for the embodiment of my experience in the rule it imposes. The best way, therefore, to make that search creative is to consult me who can alone fully report what my experience is. There can be no guarantee that law will be accepted save in the degree that this is done. Legal right is so made as the individual recipient of a command invests it with right; he gives it his sanction by relating it successfully to his own experience. When that relation cannot be made, the authority of law is always in doubt. And it is in doubt because, by contradicting the experience of those whom it seeks to control, it seems to them a frustration of their personality. To accept the control would be to become unfree.

An extreme way of putting this view would be to say that law is made by the individual's acceptance of it, that the essence of the law-making process, is the consent of interested minds. At points of marginal significance, that is, I think, true; and the consequences of the truth are obviously important. Authority, if my view is right, is always acting at its peril. It lives not by its power to command but by its power to convince. And conviction is born of consent for the simple reason that the real field of social action is in the individual

mind. Somewhere, inevitably, the power to coerce
that mind to ways of thoughts of which it does not
approve, breaks down; man, as Tyrrell said, is driven
on 'to follow the dominant influence of his life even
if it should break the heart of all the world'. That is
the stark fact which conditions the loyalty any authority
seeks to secure. At some point, it cannot be imposed
but must be won from us. And the greater the degree
in which it springs from that persuasion, the greater,
also, is the success of authority in imposing its solutions.
No power can ever hope for successful permanence, no
power, either, is entitled to it, which does not make
its way, in vital matters, through the channels of consent.

From this two conclusions seem to me to flow. Ours
is not a universe in which the principles of a unified
experience are unfolded. It is a multiverse embodying
an ultimate variety of experiences, never identical, and
always differently interpreted. There is enough similarity of view to enable us, if we have patience and
goodwill, to make enough of unity to achieve order
and peace. But that similarity is not identity. It does
not entitle us to affirm that one man's experience can
be taken as the representation of another's. It does not
justify the inference that I shall find what I most truly
desire in the desire of another. I am not a part of some
great symphony in which I realize myself only as an
incident in the *motif* of the whole. I am unique, I am
separate, I am myself; out of these qualities I must
build my own principles of action. These are mine
only, and cannot be made for me, at least creatively,
by others. For their authority as principles comes from
the fact that I recognize them as mine. Into them, as
principles, I pour my personality, and life, for me,
derives its meaning from their unique texture. To accept
the forcible imposition of other principles upon me,
which I do not recognize as the expression of my experi-

ence, is to make of me who might be free, a slave. I become an instrument of alien purposes, devoted to an end which denies my selfhood. Law, therefore, as coercion is always an invasion of personality, an abridgment of the moral stature of those whom it invades. To be true to its purpose, it must reduce the imperative element to a minimum if it is to release creativeness and not destroy it.

The individual, therefore, is entitled to act upon the judgment of his conscience in public affairs. He is entitled to assume that he will not find the rules of the conduct he ought to pursue objectified in any institution or set of institutions. I agree that, for most of us, conscience is a poor guide. It is perverse, it is foolish, the little knowledge it has is small alongside the worth of the social tradition. But perverse, foolish, ignorant, it is the only guide we have. Perverse, foolish, ignorant, it is at least ours; and our freedom comes from acting upon its demands. We ought, doubtless, to convince ourselves that the path it indicates is one we have no alternative but to follow. We ought to seek the best possible means for its instruction and enlightenment. We should remember that civilization is, at best, a fragile thing, and that to embark upon a challenge to order is to threaten what little security it has. It may even be wise, as T. H. Green once put it, to assume that we should approach the state in fear and trembling, remembering constantly the high mission with which it is charged.

All this may be true, and yet it seems to me to leave the individual no option but to follow conscience as the guide to civic action. To do otherwise is to betray freedom. Those who accept commands they know to be wrong, make it easier for wrong commands to be accepted. Those who are silent in the presence of injustice are in fact part-authors of it. It is to be remembered that even a decision to acquiesce is a decision, that what shapes the substance of authority is what it encounters. If it meets always with obedience, sooner or later it will assume its own infallibility. When that moment comes, whatever its declared purpose, the good it will seek will be in its own good and not that of those involved in its operations. Liberty means being faithful to oneself, and it is maintained by the courage to resist. This, and this only, gives life to the safeguards of liberty; and this only is the clue to the preservation of genuine integrity in the individual life.

If it is objected that this is a doctrine of contingent anarchy, that it admits the right of men to rebellion, my answer is that the accusation is true. But is its truth important? Order, surely, is not the supreme good, and rebellion has not always been wrong. Power is not conferred upon men for the sake of power, but to enable them to achieve ends which win happiness for each of us. If what they do is a denial of the purpose they serve; if, as we meet their acts, there appears in them an absence of goodwill, a blindness to experience alien from their own, an incapacity imaginatively to meet the wants of others, what alternatives have we save a challenge to power or a sacrifice of the end of our life? We do not condemn Washington because there came a moment in his career when he was compelled to recognize that the time for compromise with England had passed. We do not, even more notably, condemn those early Christians who refused to offer incense to the Gods. We have to act by the dictates of our conscience knowing, as Washington knew, as the early Christians recognized, that the penalties of failure are terrible. But we can so act, also, knowing that there is a sense in which no man who serves his conscience ever fails.

For by that service he becomes a free man, and his

freedom is a condition of other men's freedom. There is immense significance in the fact that those who fought for religious liberty were the unconscious progenitors of civil liberty also. When they demanded the right to worship the God they knew, in their own mind they were insisting that in one sphere, at least, of human experience, their own perception must count as ultimate. They consecrated freedom to the service of God. But that, after all, is only one aspect of freedom. Its consecration to the service of man is, for some of us, not less vital and pervasive. To fight for the assurance that a man may do his duty as he conceives it is not only to fight for freedom, but for all the ends which the emancipation of mankind seeks to attain. I do not know whether liberty is the highest objective we can serve. I do assert that no other great purpose is possible of achievement save in the terms of fellowship with freedom.

CHAPTER II

FREEDOM OF THE MIND

1

I HAVE sought, so far, to show that, however important be the political mechanisms on which liberty depends, they will not work of themselves. They depend for their creativeness upon the presence in any given society of a determination to make them work. The knowledge that an invasion of liberty will always meet with resistance from men determined upon its repulsion, this, in the last analysis, is the only true safeguard that we have. It means, I have admitted, that a certain penumbra of contingent anarchy always confronts the state ; but I have argued that this is entirely desirable since the secret of liberty is always, in the end, the courage to resist.

The most important aspect of this atmosphere is undoubtedly freedom of the mind. The citizen seeks for happiness, and the state, for him, is an institution which exists to make his happiness possible. He judges it, I have urged, by its capacity to respond to the needs he infers from the experience he encounters. That experience, I have insisted, is private to himself. Its predominant quality is its uniqueness. Either it is his own, or it is nothing. The substitution for it of someone else's experience, however much wider or wiser than his, is, where it is based upon constraint, a denial of freedom. What the citizen, quite rightly, expects from the state is to have his experience counted in the making of policy, and to have it counted as he, and he only, expresses its import.

Obviously enough if his experience is to count a man must be able to state it freely. The right to speak it, to print it, to seek in concert with others its translation into the event, is fundamental to liberty. If he is driven, in this realm, to silence and inactivity, he becomes a dumb and inarticulate creature, whose personality is neglected in the making of policy. Without freedom of the mind and of association a man has no means of self-protection in our social order. He may speak wrongly or foolishly ; he may associate with others for purposes that are abhorrent to the majority of men. Yet a denial of his right to do these things is a denial of his happiness. Thereby, he becomes an instrument of other people's ends, not himself an end. That is the essential condition of the perversion of power. Once we inhibit freedom of speech, we inhibit criticism of social institutions. The only opinions of which account is then taken are the opinions which coincide with the will of those in authority. Silence is taken for consent ; and the decisions that are registered as law reflect, not the total needs of the society, but the powerful needs which have been able to make themselves felt at the source of power. Historically, the road to tyranny has always lain through a denial of freedom in this realm.

I desire here to maintain a twofold thesis. I shall seek to show, first, that liberty of thought and association —the two things are inextricably intertwined—is good in itself, and second, that its denial is always a means to the preservation of some special and, usually, sinister interest which cannot maintain itself in an atmosphere of freedom. I shall then discuss what restrictions, if any, must be placed upon this right, and the conditions it demands for its maximum realization. I shall, in particular, maintain that all restrictions upon freedom of expression upon the grounds that they are seditious or blasphemous are contrary to the well-being of society.

The case for the view that freedom of thought and speech is a good in itself is fairly easy to make. If it is the business of those who exercise authority in the State to satisfy the wants of those over whom they rule, it is plain that they should be informed of those wants; and, obviously, they cannot be truly informed about them unless the mass of men is free to report their experience. No State, for instance, could rightly legislate about the hours of labour if only business men were free to offer their opinion upon industrial conditions. We could not develop an adequate law of divorce if only those happily married were entitled to express an opinion upon its terms. Law must take account of the totality of experience and this can only be known to it as that experience is unfettered in its opportunity of expression.

Most people are prepared to agree with this view when it is made as a general statement; most people, also, recoil from it when its implications are made fully known. For it implies not only the right to beautify the present social order, but the right, also, to condemn it with vigour and completeness. A man may say that England or America will never be genuinely democratic unless equality of income is established there; that equality of income may never be established except by force; that, accordingly, the way to a genuine democracy lies through a bloody revolution. Or he may argue that eternal truth is the sole possession of the Roman Catholic Church; that men can only be persuaded to understand this by the methods of the Inquisition; that, therefore, the re-establishment of the Inquisition is in the highest interest of society. To most of us, these views will seem utterly abhorrent. Yet they represent the generalizations of an experience that someone has felt. They point to needs which are seeking satisfaction, and the society gains nothing by prohibiting their expression.

For no one really ceases to be a revolutionary Communist or a passionate Roman Catholic by being forbidden to be either of these. His conviction that society is rotten at its base is only the more ardently held, his search for alternative ways of expressing his conviction becomes only the more feverish as a result of suppression. Terror does not alter opinion. On the one hand it reinforces it, on the other it makes the substance of opinion a matter of interest to many who would, otherwise, have had no interest whatever in it. When the United States Customs Department suppressed *Candide* on the ground that it was an obscene book, they merely stimulated the perverse curiosity of thousands to whom *Candide* would have remained less than a name. When the British Government prosecuted the Communists for sedition in 1925 the daily reports of the trial, the editorial discussion of its result, made the principles of Communism known to innumerable readers who would never, under other circumstances, have troubled to acquaint themselves with its nature. No State can suppress the human impulse of curiosity, and there is always a special delight, a kind of psychological scarcity-value, in knowledge of the forbidden. No technique of suppression has so far been discovered which does not have the effect of giving wider currency to the thing suppressed than can be attained in any other fashion.

But this is only the beginning of the case for freedom of speech. The heresies we may suppress today are the orthodoxies of tomorrow. New truth begins always in a minority of one; it must be someone's perception before it becomes a general perception. The world gains nothing from a refusal to entertain the possibility that a new idea may be true. Nor can we pick and choose

D

among our suppressions with any prospect of success.
It would, indeed, be hardly beyond the mark to affirm
that a list of the opinions condemned as wrong or
dangerous would be a list of the commonplaces of our
time. Most people can see that Nero and Diocletian
accomplished nothing by their persecution of Christianity. But every argument against their attitude is an
argument also against a similar attitude in other persons.
Upon what grounds can we infer prospective gain from
persecution of opinion? If the view held is untrue,
experience shows that conviction of its untruth is invariably a matter of time; it does not come because
authority announces that it is untrue. If the view is
true in part only, the separation of truth and falsehood
is accomplished most successfully in a free intellectual
competition, a process of dissociation by rational
criticism, in which those who hold the false opinion
are driven to defend their position on rational grounds.
If, again, the view held is wholly true, nothing whatever is gained by preventing its expression. Whether
it relates to property, or marriage, to religion or the
form of the State, by being true it demands a corres-
ponding change in individual outlook and social organization. For untrue opinions do not permanently
work. They impede discovery and they diminish happiness. They enable, of course, those to whom they are
profitable, to benefit by their maintenance, but it is at
the cost of society as a whole.

There is the further question, moreover, of the persons to whom the task of selecting what should be
suppressed is to be confided. What qualifications are
they to possess for their task? What tests are they to
apply from which the desirability of suppression is to
be inferred? A mere zeal for the well-being of society
is an utterly inadequate qualification; for most persons
who have played the part of censor have possessed this

and have yet been utterly unfit for their task. The self-appointed person, Mr. Comstock, for instance, merely identifies his private view of moral right with the ultimate principles of ethics; and only the intellectually blind would ask that the citizen be fitted to his vicious bed of Procrustes. The official censor, a man like the famous Pobedonostev, normally assumes that any thorough criticism of the existing social order is dangerous and destructive; and, thereby, he transforms what might be creative demand into secret attack which is ten times more dangerous in its influence. If you take almost any of those who are appointed to work of this kind, you discover that association with it seems necessarily to unfit them for their task. For it turns them into men who see undesirability in work which the average man reads without even a suspicion that it is not the embodiment of experience with which he ought to be acquainted. Anyone who looks through the list of prohibited publications enforced by the Dominion of Canada will, I think, get a sense that the office of censorship is the avenue to folly.[1] No one with whom I am acquainted seems wise enough or good enough to control the intellectual nutrition of the human mind.

What tests, further, are they to apply? Broadly speaking, we suppress publications on the ground that they are obscene or dangerous. But no one has ever arrived at a working definition of obscenity, even for legal purposes. Take, for instance, two books suppressed by the English magistrates for obscenity in 1929. One, Miss Radclyffe Hall's *Well of Loneliness*, seemed to men like Mr. Arnold Bennett and Mr. Bernard Shaw a work which treated of a theme of high importance to society in a sober and high-minded way. They saw no reason to suppose that the treatment of its difficult

[1] A list is printed in Ernst and Segal, *To the Pure* (1929), pp. 296–302.

subject—sexual perversion—could be regarded by any
normal person as offensive. The magistrate, Sir Chartres
Biron, took a different view. I, certainly, am not prepared, on *a priori* grounds, to say that a lawyer, however well trained in the law, has a better sense of what
is likely to produce moral depravity than Mr. Bennett
or Mr. Shaw; and a reading of Miss Hall's dull and
sincere pamphlet only reinforces that impression.
Another book was distributed privately and secretly—
Mr. D. H. Lawrence's *Lady Chatterley's Lover*—in a
limited and expensive special edition. I gather that its
public sale would have been definitely prohibited. Yet
I observe that some of the most eminent American
critics have praised it as the finest example of a novel
seeking the truth about the sexual relations of men and
women that an Englishman has published in the twentieth
century. That may be—I am not competent to say—
excessive praise. My point is that in a choice, say,
between the average police magistrate and Mr. Robert
Morass Lovett, I am not prepared to accept the former's
opinion of what I may be safely left to read.

Let me remind you, moreover, of what cannot too
often be pointed out, that the rigorous application of
the legal tests of obscenity would prohibit the circulation of a very considerable part of the great literature
of the world. The Bible, Shakespeare, Rabelais, Plato,
Horace, Catullus, to take names at random, would all
come under the ban. It is worth while pointing out
that those most concerned with the suppression of
'obscene' books are religious people. On their tests of
obscenity the Bible certainly could not hope to escape;
yet they believe, in general, that the Bible is the inspired
word of God, a position which, I venture to suggest,
should at the least give them pause. I do not know,
indeed, how we are to create a healthy social attitude
to the problems of sex, if all that deals with it from a

new point of view, and with a frankness that admits
the experimental nature of our contemporary solutions, is to be dismissed as 'obscene'. Questions like
those of birth control, extra-marital love, companionate
marriage, sexual perversion, cannot really be faced in
a scientific fashion by applying to them the standards
of a nomadic Eastern people which drew up its rules
more than two thousand years ago. Virtuous people
who shrink from frank discussion in this realm seem
to me responsible for probably more gratuitous suffering than any other group of human beings. The thing
they call 'innocence' I believe to be quite wanton
ignorance, and, by its abridgment of freedom, it imprisons human personality in a fashion that is quite
unpardonable.

The same seems to me to be the case in the realm
that is called blasphemy. I have no sort of sympathy
with that attitude of mind which finds satisfaction in
wanton insult to the religious convictions of others.
But I am not prepared for its suppression. For I note
that, historically, there are no limits to the ideas which
religious persons will denounce as blasphemous; and,
especially, that in an age of comparative religious
indifference, the hand of persecution almost invariably
chooses to fall only on humble men.[1] It attacks Mr.
G. W. Foote, but it leaves Lord Morley free to do
infinitely more damage than any for which Mr. Foote
can ever have been responsible. I cannot, moreover,
forget that what is blasphemy in Tennessee is common
sense in New York, that the works of Wollaston and
Toland and Chubb, which seemed entirely blasphemous
to their generation, seem commonplace to ourselves.
Every religious body really means by blasphemy an
attack upon its fundamental principles. Such attacks

[1] This is brought out well in Mr. Nokes' excellent book on
the blasphemy laws.

are, of course, necessarily circulated to bring them into
contempt. We who read Paine's *Age of Reason* with
admiration for its cogency of argument, its trenchant
style, its fearless appetite for truth, can hardly avoid a
sense of dismay when we remember the days when it
was secretly passed from hand to hand as an outrageous production, the possession of which was itself
an indication of social indecency.

And here let me remind you of certain facts on the
other side. We denominate as blasphemous works
calculated to bring the principles of Christianity into
hatred, ridicule, or contempt. As I have said, I entirely
dislike the type of work which finds pleasure in offen-
siveness to Christians. But if we are to suppress works,
and punish their authors, because they cause grief to
certain of our fellow-citizens, exactly how far are we
to carry the principle? A very large part of propa-
gandist religious literature is highly offensive to sincere
and serious-minded persons who are unable, in their
conscience, to subscribe to any particular creed. When
you remember the descriptions applied by Mr. William
Sunday to those who do not accept Christianity, you
cannot, I think, avoid a sense that there is a religious
blasphemy for which, at least from the angle of good
manners, nothing whatever can be said. Mr. Sunday
is only one of the worse offenders in a whole tribe of
preachers and writers to whom belief, however sincere,
that is alien from their own, is normally and naturally
described in the language it is a euphemism to call
Billingsgate; and charges of immorality are brought
against unbelievers by them for which not an atom of
proof exists. Are we to suppress all such publications
also? And if we are to continue this campaign of
prohibition to its appointed and logical end, shall we
have time for any other social adventure?

Nor is this all. In the world of education we are

continually presented with the problem of text-books
which are offensive to a particular denomination. We
are asked, for instance, to prohibit their use in schools.
I sit as an appointed member of the Education Committee of the London County Council. I have been
presented there with a requisitory, drawn up by a
Catholic body, against the use of certain books on the
ground that they contain untrue statements about questions like the Reformation, in which Catholics are
particularly interested. But I have not observed in the
same Catholic body a desire only to use those text-
books in their own denominational schools which
Protestants are prepared to accept as a true picture of
the Reformation. Nor is this problem of school text-
books merely religious in character. Americans of our
own generation have seen passionate controversy over
the view of the War of Independence, of the Constitution, of the motives and responsibility in the war of
1914, which are to be presented not merely to school
children, but also to university students; there is a
heresy-hunt in the fields of politics and economics, a
desire to have only 'true' opinions taught to the im-
mature mind. But 'true' opinions, on examination,
usually turn out to be the opinions which suit the pro-
ponents of some particular cause. In London we think
that a 'true' theory of value is best obtained from the
works of Professor Cannan; in Cambridge they pin
their faith to Marshall and Pigou; in the Labour
Colleges ultimate wisdom is embodied in the writings
of Marx, and Cannan, Marshall and Pigou are all dismissed as the pathetic servants of bourgeois capitalism.
Is anything gained for anyone by insisting that truth
resides on one side only of a particular Pyrénées? Is
it not wisdom to begin by an admission of its many-
sidedness? And does not that admission involve an
unlimited freedom of expression in the interpretation

of facts? For facts, as William James said, are not
born free and equal. They have to be interpreted in
the light of our experience; and to suppress someone's
experience is to suppress someone's personality, to
impose upon him our view of what his life implies to
the forcible exclusion of that in which alone he can
find meaning. I see neither wisdom nor virtue in action
of this kind.

So far, I have restricted my discussion to the non-
political field, and before I enter this area, I want, for
a moment, both to summarize the position we have
reached and to admit the one limitation on freedom
of expression I am prepared to concede. I have denied
that prohibitions arising from blasphemy or obscenity,
or historical or social unfairness, have any justification.
They seem to me unworkable. They are bad because
they prevent necessary social ventilation. They are bad
because they exclude the general public from access
to facts and ideas which are often of vital importance.
They are bad because no one is wise or virtuous enough
to stand in judgment upon what another man is to
think or say or write. They are bad because they are
incapable of common-sense application; there is never
any possibility of a wise discrimination in their application. They give excessive protection to old traditions;
they make excessively difficult the entrance of new.
They confer power in a realm where qualifications for
the exercise of power, and tests for its application, are,
almost necessarily, non-existent. For the decision of
every question of this kind is a matter of opinion in
which there is no prospect of certainty. Suppression
here means not the prohibition of the untrue or the
unjust or the immoral, but of opinions unpleasing to
those who exercise the censorship. Historically, no
evidence exists to suggest that it has ever been exercised
for other ends.

I do not see any rational alternative to this view. But here I should emphasize my own belief that, broadly speaking, such freedom of expression as I have discussed means freedom to express one's ideas on general subjects, on themes of public importance, rather than on the character of particular persons. I have not, I think, a right to suggest that Jones beats his wife, or that Brown continually cheats his employer, unless I can prove, first that the suggestions are true, and, second, that they have a definite public import. I have not a right to create scandal because I find pleasure or profit in speaking ill of my neighbour. But if Brown, for instance, is a candidate for public office, my view that he cheats his employer is directly relevant to the question of his fitness to be elected; and if I can prove that my view is true, it is in the public interest that I should make it known. I cannot, that is to say, regard my freedom of expression as unlimited. I ought not to be permitted to inflict unnecessary pain on any person unless there is relevant social welfare in that infliction.

On the other hand, I would make one remark here that seems to me of increasing importance in a society like our own. The public interest in the habits of individuals is real, and we must be careful to give it its proper protection. It is, I think, reasonable to doubt whether the Anglo-American law of libel, in its present state, does not push too far the right of the individual citizen to be protected from comment. Outrageous damages, which bear no measurable relation to anything, are often claimed and not seldom awarded. Where a political flavour enters into a case, it is difficult, and sometimes impossible, to persuade a jury to consider the issue on its merits. I have myself sat on a jury in a political libel case of which I can only say that I was almost persuaded to doubt the validity of

the jury-system altogether by the habits there displayed.
I am tempted to suggest that, criminal libel apart, it
would be worth while considering the abolition of
damages in all political or quasi-political cases, and
the concentration, as an alternative, upon proper publicity for the form of apology where the libel is held
to be proved. We have, for instance, got into the bad
habit in England of thinking that the social position
of the plaintiff is a measure of the damages he should
receive; and it is well known that there are places
where, for instance, a socialist could hardly hope even
for a verdict from any average jury. The case for careful
inquiry, at any rate, seems to me to be made out. As
the law at present stands and works, I do not think
I could even say of a candidate for the House of Commons that he was not likely to be more than a permanent
back-bencher without having to pay heavily for my
opinion.

II

But I turn from these relatively simple matters to
the political aspect of freedom of expression which is,
of course, the pith of the whole problem. How far is
a man entitled to go in an attack upon the social order?
What opinions, if any, are to be prohibited on the
ground that they incite to subversive conduct? Is there
a distinction between the printed word and the spoken
word? Is there a distinction between speech in one
place, and speech in another? Is there a difference
between normal times and a time of crisis like, let us
say, a war or a general strike? At what point, if any,
do words become acts of which authority must take
account to fulfil its primary duty of maintaining the
peace?

It will, I think, be universally agreed that all criticism
of social institutions is a matter of degree. Let us take
the problem first as we meet it in normal times and let

us view it from the angle of the English law of sedition.[1]
Here it may be said at once that were that law enforced
in its literal terms, political controversy in England
would be impossible. For the declared purpose of the
law is to prevent the established institutions of the
State from being brought into hatred or contempt, and
every leader of the opposition is seeking to do precisely that thing when he makes a political speech.
Anyone who reads, for instance, the utterances of
Lord Carson at the time of the Home Rule fight in
1914, or of Mr. Ramsay MacDonald in the General
Election of 1929, cannot avoid the conclusion that,
taken literally, they were seditious. Yet all of us agree
that it is not the purpose of the law to prevent such
speeches being made. When, therefore, if ever, is that
law to be brought into operation?

We must, I think, begin by a distinction between the
written and the spoken word. If an English Communist
leader writes a book or pamphlet, whatever its substance, and to whomever it is addressed, I do not think
the law ought to be used against him. For it is the
history of these matters that if governments once begin
to prohibit men from seeking to prove in writing that
violent revolution is desirable, they will, sooner or
later, prohibit them from saying that the social order
they represent is not divine. In Italy, at the moment,
for example, papers are actually suppressed not for
anything positive that they say, but because there is
absent from their pages frequent and emphatic eulogy
of the present régime; there have even been calls for
suppression because particular papers, while saying no
word against Mussolini, have been too insistently
eulogistic of the Papacy. I yield to no one in my dissent from, say, Lenin's analysis of the nature of the
modern State. But I think it urgent that his criticism

[1] 53 Geo. III, c. 160.

should be available to society. For it represents the impress made upon him by the experience of political life, and a government which remains unaware of that criticism has lost its chance of seeking to satisfy the critic. If it begins by assuming that the exposition of Revolutionary Communism is undesirable, it will end, as the record shows, that language classes to teach English to Russians are a form of Communist propaganda. There is never any such certitude in matters of social constitution as to justify us in saying that any exposition of principles must be suppressed. No authority has ever a capacity for wise discrimination in these matters; and, even if it had, I do not see why it is justified in the exercise of discrimination.

For suppression, in the first place, never convinces. What it does is to drive a small body of men to desperation and to reduce the masses to complete apathy in political matters. Most men who are prohibited from thinking as their experience teaches them soon cease to think at all. Men who cease to think cease also in any genuine sense to be citizens. They become the mere inert recipients of orders which they obey without scrutiny of any kind. And their inertia surrounds the acts of authority with that false glamour of confidence which mistakes silence for consent. The government which is not criticized at its base never truly knows the sentiments to which its activity gives rise among its subjects. It ultimately must fail to satisfy them because it does not know what desires it has to satisfy. Political thought, after all, however unwise or mistaken, is never born in a vacuum. Lenin's view of capitalist society is just as relevant to its habits as the view of the Duke of Northumberland or of Judge Gary; each is born of contact with it, and each, as it is expressed, has lessons to teach from which, as these are scrutinized, a wise policy can be born.

Here, I think, it is relevant to say a word upon one special aspect of freedom of expression for printed matter. I have argued that no limit of any kind is to be placed upon it, at any rate in normal times. The book, the pamphlet and the newspaper ought to circulate with unimpeded freedom in whatever direction they can move. Many people who sympathize with this view will, however, except from this freedom printed material which is addressed to the armed forces of the State; and most governments, of course, have special legislation, with specially severe penalties, against any attempt at interference with their loyalty. I cannot myself see that this exception is justified. The armed forces of the State consist of citizens. The government has quite exceptional opportunities to retain their allegiance. If a printed document is able to sow disaffection amongst them, there must be something very wrong with the government. And, in fact, whenever agitation has produced military or naval disloyalty that has been the outcome not of affection for the principles upon which the agitators lay emphasis, but of grievances which have made either soldiers or sailors responsive to a plea for their disloyalty. That was the case with the Spithead mutinies of 1797; with the French troops in 1789; with the Russian troops in 1917. If the army or the navy is prepared to turn upon the government, the likelihood is great that the government is unfit to retain power. For anyone who can disturb the allegiance of a mind as trained to obedience as that of the soldier or the sailor has, I believe, an *a priori* case for insisting that his particular philosophy corresponds to an urgent human need.

It is said that ideas are explosive and dangerous. To allow them unfettered freedom is, in fact, to invite disorder. But, to this position, there are at least two final answers. It is impossible to draw a line round

dangerous ideas, and any attempt at their definition
involves monstrous folly. If views, moreover, which
imply disorder are able to disturb the foundations of
the State, there is something supremely wrong with
the governance of that State. For disorder is not a
habit of mankind. We cling so eagerly to our accustomed ways that, as even Burke insisted, popular
violence is always the outcome of a deep popular sense
of wrong. The common man can only be persuaded
to outbreak, granted his general habits, when the
government of the State has lost its hold upon his
affections; and that loss is always the reflection of a
profound moral cause. We may, indeed, go further
and argue that the best index to the quality of a State
is the degree in which it is able to permit free criticism
of itself. For that implies an alertness to public opinion,
a desire to remedy grievance, which enables the State
to gain ground in the allegiance of its citizens. Almost
always freedom of speech results in a mitigation which
renders disorder unnecessary; almost always, also,
prohibition of that freedom merely makes the agitation
more dangerous because it drives it underground.
Rousseau was infinitely more dangerous as a persecuted
wanderer, because infinitely more interesting and, therefore, infinitely more persuasive, than he would have
been when unfettered in Paris. Lenin did far more
harm to Russia as an exile in Switzerland than he could
ever have accomplished as an opposition leader in the
Duma. The right freely to publish the written word
is, in fact, the supreme katharsis of discontent. Governments that are wise can always learn more from the
criticism of their opponents than they can hope to
discover in the eulogies of their friends. When they
stifle that criticism, they prepare the way for their own
destruction.

There is, I think, an undeniable difference between

freedom of written and freedom of spoken, expression.
In the one case, a man attempts conviction by individual
persuasion; he seeks, by argument which he believes
to be rational, to move the mind of those who read
what he has written. To speak at a meeting raises
different problems. No one with experience of a great
crowd under the sway of a skilled orator can doubt
his power deliberately to create disorder if he so desires.
A speaker at Trafalgar Square, for instance, who urged
a vast meeting of angry unemployed to march on
Downing Street, could do so with a fair assurance
that they would obey his behest. I do not think a
government can be left to the not always tender mercies
of an orator with a grievance to exploit. The State,
clearly, has the right to protection against the kind
of public utterance which is bound to result in disorder.

But no government is entitled itself to assume that
disorder is imminent: the proof must be offered to an
independent authority. And the proof so offered must
be evidence that the utterance to which it takes
exception was, at the time and in the circumstances
in which it was made, definitely calculated to result
in a breach of the peace. Its prohibitions must not
be preventive prohibitions. It must not prohibit a
meeting before it is held on the ground that the speaker
is likely to preach sedition there. It must not seek
conviction for sedition where the utterance might,
under other circumstances, have had the tendency to
result in a breach of the peace. To use my earlier
illustration, I think a government would be justified
in prosecution of the Trafalgar Square orator; but I
do not think it would be entitled to prosecute the same
speaker if he made the same speech on Calton Hill
in Edinburgh. For we know that when men in Edinburgh
are incited to march on London, they have a habit
of turning back at Derby. I conclude, therefore, that

the test adopted by Mr. Justice Holmes, in his deservedly famous dissent in *Abrams* v. *U.S.*,[1] is the maximum prohibition a government can be permitted. If it is in fact demonstrable that the speech made had a direct tendency to incite immediate disorder, the punishment of the accused is justified. I think such cases should always be tried before a jury. Experience suggests that a random sample of popular opinions is more likely to do justice in this type of case than is a judge. I have myself been present at such trials before a magistrate where the whole case for the prosecution quite obviously broke down and where, nevertheless, a conviction was secured. I do not for a moment suggest that we can be confident that a jury will act wisely; but my sense of our experience is that there is less chance of its acting unwisely than persons who occupy an official position of any kind. With the best will in the world, their tendency is to be unduly responsive to executive opinion.

You will see that my anxiety is to maximize the difficulties of any government which desires to initiate prosecutions in this realm. My reason for this view is the quite simple one that I do not trust the executive power to act wisely in the presence of any threat, nor assumed threat, to public order. Anyone who studies the treason trials of 1794, or, even more striking, the cases under the Espionage Act in America during 1917–20, will be convinced of the unwisdom of allowing the executive an undue latitude. Every State contains innumerable and stupid men who see in unconventional thought the imminent destruction of social peace. They become Ministers; and they are quite capable of thinking that a society of Tolstoyan anarchists is about to attempt a new gunpowder plot. If you think of men like Lord Eldon, like Sir William Joynson-Hicks, like Attorney-

[1] *Ut supra.*

General Palmer, you will realize how natural it is for them to believe that the proper place for Thoreau or Tolstoy, for William Morris or Mr. Bernard Shaw, is a prison. I am unable to take that view; and I am therefore anxious that they should not be able to make it prevail without finding that there are barriers in their path.

III

Views such as I have put forward are often regarded with sympathy when their validity is limited to normal times. In a crisis, it is argued, different considerations prevail. When the safety of a State is threatened it is bound to take, and is justified in taking, all action to end the crisis. To suggest that it should be then bound by principles which weaken its effective striking power, is, it is said, to ask it to fight with one hand tied behind its back. The first objective of any society must be organized security; it is only when this has been obtained, that freedom of speech is within the pale of discussion.

I am unable to share this view. We have really to examine two quite different positions. There is, first, the question of the principles to be applied in a period of internal violence; there is, next, the quite special question of limitation upon utterance in a period of war. I agree at once that it is entirely academic to demand freedom of speech in a time of civil war, for the simple reason that no one will pay the slightest attention to the demand; violence and freedom are, *a priori*, contradictory terms. But I would point out two things. In general, revolutions fail because those who make them deny freedom to their opponents. Losing criticism, they do not know the limits within which they can safely operate; they lose their power because they are not told when they are abusing it. I can think of no revolutionary period in history when a government has gained by stifling the opinion of men who did not see eye to eye with it; and I suggest that the revolutionary insistence that persuasion is futile finds little creative evidence in its support.

But when once the question has been settled of who is to possess power other questions of urgent delicacy arise in which, as I think, the principles I have laid down possess an irresistible force. There is the problem of how the rebel and the disaffected are to be treated; of whether the resumption of order is to be followed by free discussion; of the power to be exercised by the military authority over ordinary citizens not engaged in armed hostility to the régime. Here I can only express the view that the resumption of order ought always to be followed forthwith by the normal principles of judicial control; and that the military authorities ought not, save where it is quite impossible for the civil courts to exercise their jurisdiction, to have any powers over ordinary citizens.

These are rigorous views; and, perhaps, I may devote a little time to their exposition. I know of no case where the State has exercised extraordinary power outside the normal process of law, in which that authority has not been grossly abused. It was abused in the Civil War even under a mind so humane and generous as that of Lincoln; it was emphatically and dangerously abused in the Amritsar rebellion of 1919. Let me illustrate, from this latter example, some of the things that were done. Two men were arrested in Amritsar prior to the declaration of martial law and deported to an extreme and undisturbed part of the province; on the declaration of martial law, they were brought back to Lahore, which was in the martial law area, and tried and sentenced by a martial law tribunal. A number of pleaders were arrested in Gudaspur, where there was no disturbance, taken under revolting conditions to Lahore, and confined there in the common jail for a period lasting up to a month. They were then released, without any charges being preferred against them; on the evidence, indeed, it is difficult to know with what offence they could have been charged. In the trial, again, of one Harkishan Lal, and others, for treason and waging war against the King-Emperor, the accused were not allowed to have a lawyer of their own choosing; a full record of the case was not taken, and the private notes of counsel for the defence had to be surrendered by him to the Court at the end of each day. Under such conditions it is difficult to see how any adequate defence was possible. A punitive detachment, again, under a Colonel Jacob, tried by drumhead court-martial, and flogged, a man who refused, it appears with some truculence, to say who had destroyed some telegraph wires; later it appeared that the man, as he had asserted, had in fact no knowledge of who had destroyed them. In Lahore—to take a final instance—the military officer in command prohibited more than a few persons to congregate in the streets; a few persons did so congregate and they were flogged. On investigation, after the flogging, it was found that the group was a wedding-party whose purpose was not more dangerous than that of any other persons engaged in a similar function.[1]

I do not, of course, suggest that there is anything especially cruel or remarkable in these instances. Whether you study repression in Ireland or Russia, Bavaria or Hungary or India, its history is always the same. The fact always emerges that once the operation of justice is transferred from the ordinary courts to some branch of the executive, abuses always occur. The proper protection of the individual is deliberately neglected in the belief that a reign of terror will minimize disaffection. There is no evidence that it does. If it could,

[1] Cf. my *Grammar of Politics*, p. 554.

there would have been no Russian Revolution; and there would be no movement for Indian self-government today. The error inherent in any invasion of individuality, such as a system of special courts implies, is that it blinds the eyes of government to the facts not only by suppressing illegitimate expression of opinion, but by persuading it that most opinion which finds expression is illegitimate if it is not in the nature of eulogy. Even Lincoln supported his generals in completely indefensible attacks on civilian rights. Executive justice, in fact, is simply a euphemism for the denial of justice; and the restoration of order at this cost involves dangers of which the price is costly indeed.

The problem of war is, in a sense, a special case of the problem of disorder; but, in fact, it raises quite different considerations. Let me first of all make the point that if you are a citizen in a besieged town, you cannot expect a normal freedom of speech; to be within the area of actual military operations means that you must not hope to be regarded as an individual. You become, from the nature of things, a unit of attack or defence whose personality is immaterial and insignificant. The position here is extraordinary; and principles have little or no relation to the problems that arise. The case, as elsewhere, merely affords proof that liberty and violence are antithetic terms.

But let us rather take the position of a citizen whose country is involved in war as, say, England in 1914, or America in 1917. What are his rights and duties then? I would begin by making the point that the fact of belligerency does not suspend his citizenship; he owes as much, perhaps more than ever, the contribution his instructed judgment can make, to the public good. The scale of operations cannot, I think, make any difference to that duty. It is as real, and as compelling, when they are big, as in the war of 1914, as when, as in the Boer War, or the Spanish-American War, they are relatively small. If I think the war a just one, it is my duty to support it, and if I think it unjust there is no alternative open to me except opposition to it. I believe, for instance, that the opposition of Mr. Ramsay MacDonald and Mr. Snowden to the war of 1914 was a fulfilment, on their part, of the highest civil obligation. No citizen can assume that his duty in wartime is so to abdicate the exercise of his judgment that the executive has a blank cheque to act as it pleases. No government, therefore, is entitled to penalize opinion at a time when it is more than ever urgent to perform the task of citizenship. If a man sincerely thinks, like James Russell Lowell, that war is merely an alias for murder, it is his duty to say so even if his pronouncement is inconvenient to the government of the day.

I cannot, indeed, believe that there is any case on the other side worthy of serious consideration. In the war of 1914, it was said that hostile opinion must be controlled because it hinders the successful prosecution of the war. But behind the façade of prejudice contained in the imputation of a term like hostility, there are several issues each one of which requires analysis. For what does 'hostile opinion' mean? Does it imply hostility to the inception of a war, to the methods of its prosecution, to the end at which it aims, to the terms on which its conclusion is proposed? In the war of 1914, the critics were divided into camps on each of these views. There were men, like Mr. MacDonald, who thought the war unjustified in its inception and bad in its conclusion. There were others who criticized the manner, both diplomatic and technical, of its prosecution. Was it, for instance, hostility to the prosecution of the late war to criticize Lord Jellicoe's conduct at the Battle of Jutland, or Sir Ian Hamilton's handling of the operations at the Dardanelles? Was it, again, hostility on the part of *The Times* to attack the Asquith Government on the ground, rightly or wrongly, that it showed a lack of energy in building up a munitions supply? If a statesman not in office, Mr. Roosevelt, for example, thinks the diplomatic policy of the executive likely to be attended by fatal results, must he confine himself to private representations, lest public utterance hinder the national unity? If an Englishman like Lord Lansdowne believed, as President Wilson believed in 1916, that peace by negotiation is preferable to peace by victory in the field, because of the human cost that victory entails, has he no obligation to his fellow-citizens who are paying that cost with their lives?

It is evident from our experience that to limit the expression of opinion in wartime to opinion which does not hinder its prosecution is, in fact, to give the executive an entirely free hand, whatever its policy, and to assume that, while the armies are in the field, an absolute moral moratorium is imperative. That is, surely, a quite impossible position. No one who has watched at all carefully the process of governance in time of war can doubt that criticism was never more necessary. Its limitation is, in fact, an assurance that mistakes will be made and wrong done. For once the right to criticize is withdrawn, the executive commits all the natural follies of dictatorship. It assumes a semi-divine character for its acts. It deprives the people of information essential to a proper judgment of its policy. It misrepresents the situation it confronts by that art of propaganda which, as Mr. Cornford has happily said, enables it to deceive its friends without deceiving its enemies. A people in wartime is always blind to the facts of its position and anxious to believe only agreeable news; the government takes care to provide it only with news that is pleasant. If no such news is at hand it will be manufactured. Petty successes will

be magnified into resounding victories; defeats will be
minimized, wherever possible. The agony of the troops
will be obscured by the clouds of censorship. A wartime
government is always obtuse to suggestion, angry when
inquiry is suggested, careless of truth. It can, in fact,
only be moralized to the degree to which it is subject
to critical examination in every aspect of its policy.
And to penalize, therefore, the critic is not only to
poison the moral foundations of the State, but to make
it extremely difficult, when peace comes, for both
government and the mass of citizens to resume the
habits of normal decency.

Freedom of speech, therefore, in wartime seems to
me broadly to involve the same rights as freedom of
speech in peace. It involves them, indeed, more fully
because a period of national trial is one when, above
all, it is the duty of citizens to bear their witness. I do
not, of course, mean that a citizen in wartime should
be free to communicate secret military plans to the
enemy; I do mean that if a man feels, like Sir Henry
Campbell-Bannerman, that British policy in South
Africa is 'methods of barbarism', it is his right, as
well as his duty, to say so. Obviously critical activity
of this kind will be unpopular and a government which
helps in the making of its unpopularity will find the
task of suppression easy. But it will pay a heavy price
for suppression. The winged words of criticism scatter,
only too often, the seeds of peace. Sir Henry Campbell-
Bannerman's attack on the Balfour Government persuaded General Botha that trust in Great Britain
might not be misplaced; President Wilson's speeches,
especially his Fourteen Points, were, impliedly, a
criticism of Allied policy, and that which, also, awakened
liberal opinion in Germany to a sense of its responsi-
bilities. Wartime unity of outlook, in a word, is never
worth the cost of prohibitions. If the policy of a State

which decides upon war does not command the general
assent of citizens, it has no right to make war. If the
number of those hostile is considerable, the policy is,
at the least, a dubious one. If the number is small,
there is no need to attempt suppression in the interest
of success. The only way, in fact, to attain the right is
by free discussion; and a period of crisis, when the
perception of right is difficult, only makes the emphasis
upon freedom more fundamental.

Let me illustrate my view with reference to one or
two of the decisive factors in the Peace of Versailles.
No one now believes the wartime lie that Germany
was solely responsible for the war; her responsibility
may be greater than that of some others, but it is agreed
that the burden of Russia is at least as heavy and that
war, in any case, was rooted in the nature of the
European system. But, in the interest of national
unity, it was regarded as essential to represent Germany
as the sole conspirator against European peace. She
was painted as a malefactor whose sins were incapable
of exaggeration. Her virtues were denied, her achievements belittled, until what Mr. Lippmann terms a
'stereotype' of her was built up for public use which
made her appear to the average man a criminal who
could not be too severely punished. The statesmen
who constructed this stereotype knew that it was untrue;
but they hoped, doubtless, to escape its consequences,
when the victory had been won. They found that they
could not do so. They had so successfully repressed
all effort at reasonable delineation, that the atmosphere
of hate was unconquerable. They had no alternative
to a Carthaginian peace because that seemed, to the
masses they had deceived, the only possible course for
justice to take. They knew, as the famous memorandum,
for instance, of Mr. Lloyd George makes manifest,[1]

[1] Cd. 1614 (1922).

that a Carthaginian peace was disastrous for Europe; but it was too late to destroy the legend they had created. Like those whom Dante describes in the Inferno, they were punished by the realization of their announced desires.

The world, in this context, has paid the price for the suppression of truth; and another phase of the suppression should also be remembered. It is usually agreed that some of the worst elements in the Peace of Versailles were the result of the Secret Treaties by which the Allies, exclusive of America, bound themselves to each other before the entrance of America into the war. Nowhere among the associated Powers was the desire for a just peace more widespread than in America; nowhere, also, was the discussion of war-aims more rigorously curtailed as a hindrance to the full prosecution of the war. Had discussion of the peace been full and effective in those critical years, the liberal instincts of President Wilson might, when reinforced by the weight of informed opinion, have compelled at least a considerable mitigation of the secret treaties. They had been published in the American Press after their issue by the Bolsheviks in 1917; full discussion would have revealed their inadequacies, and enabled the President to counteract what there was of evil in their substance. But the destruction of free opinion acted as a smoke-screen to conceal them, and Mr. Wilson did not seriously give his mind to them until he reached Paris. It was then too late to undo their consequences. Here, in fact, as elsewhere, uncontrolled power acted like a miasma to blot out the only atmosphere in which truth could be made manifest. No government was compelled to do its duty, because the means were wanting to inform it of what its duty was. The powers had forgotten, or had chosen to forget, that they could not hope for a just peace save by freeing the minds of men and women who cared for justice.

IV

So far, I have considered freedom in the political sphere as though it concerned only a single individual placed over against society and the State. I have sought to discuss what his freedom means in the complex relationships in which he is involved. But, obviously, this is an undue simplification of the problem. The individual, in fact, does not stand alone; he joins hands with others of like mind to persuade, sometimes to compel, society to the adoption of the view they share. It is unnecessary for me to emphasize the vital part played by associations in the modern community.[1] Granted that they have their dangers, they are not only a vital expression of human personality, but an expression as natural as the state itself. That a man must be free to combine with his fellows for joint-action in some realm in which they have a kindred interest is, I take it, of the essence of liberty. The point it is important to examine is the degree of control, if any, that the State is entitled to exercise over voluntary associations.

Let me say at once that I know no question more difficult in the whole range of political science. I am quite certain that, from the angle of individual freedom, the less interference the State attempts, the better for everyone concerned; but, equally, I am clear that to some interference the State is fully entitled. I should deny, for instance, the right of any voluntary association to inflict physical punishment or imprisonment upon its members; and I should argue that any state was justified in immediate and drastic interference to this end. But the real problems we encounter are not so simple as this. Joseph Smith announces his reception of a message from Heaven ordaining the duty of men

[1] Cf. my *Grammar of Politics*, pp. 256 ff.

to practise polygamy in a community where the law
only recognizes monogamy; what rights of interference
has the State when a body of men and women join
him and begin to give effect to his teaching? What
are the rights of the State when a congress of trade
unionists declares a general strike? Are those rights
different when the purpose of the strike is industrial
from what they are if it is political? How are we to
distinguish between the two? What are the rights of
combination among men employed in industries the
nature of which makes the service they perform fundamental to the community? What should be the attitude
of the State to a society of men engaged in propaganda
for a revolution by the use of physical force? Is there
a difference between such a society when it merely
preaches the desirability of such a revolution and when
it acts to that end? Does action, in the latter case,
mean embarkation upon rebellion, for example, the
purchase of machine-guns, or does it extend, say, to
the stirring-up of industrial strife in the hope that a
resort to political rebellion may be its outcome?

You will see that these are not merely academic
questions; every one of them has been in the forefront
of political discussion this last half-century, and all
save the first have been vital themes of decision in the
years since the war. Let us take first the case of an
association which, like the Mormon Church, desires
to practise modes of conduct different from those pursued
by the society as a whole. We have to assume that the
members of the association have joined it voluntarily,
and continue voluntarily in its membership. We have
to assume, further, that they do not desire to force
their particular way of life upon others; for some single
realm of conduct, like the realm of marriage, they desire
that they shall be left free from interference by the
organized power of society. I cannot see that we are

entitled to interfere with them. We may think them
unwise, foolish, muddle-headed, immoral. We know
perfectly well that we cannot hope, by the external
constraint of law, to abolish all conduct that comes
within those terms. I happen to think that it is a gross
superstition to leave money to the Roman Catholic
Church that masses may be said for the testator's soul;
but I should think it an unwarrantable interference
with the relations between that Church and its members
if such bequests were forbidden. I see no evidence to
suggest that the practice of polygamy is worse, in its
nature, than a hundred other practices which organized
society either directly permits, or wisely leaves alone,
because it knows that rigorous control would be utterly
futile. The only way to deal with the ideals of the
Mormon Church is to prove their undesirability to their
members. On the evidence of history, persecution will
not be acceptable as proof; and it is not improbable
that the only legal effect of prohibition has been to
make furtive and dishonest what was, at first, open
and avowed. *Mutatis mutandis*, this seems to me the
case with all similar problems of association. If a society
of women, enthusiastic for the independence of their
sex, formed themselves into an association to propagate
and practise the (to them) ideal of children outside the
tie of marriage, I should not think the State entitled
to interfere with its work. So, too, I should argue,
with a principle like birth-control. The State is not
entitled to prohibit diffusion of such knowledge, or
the practice of it. When it does, it makes the family
nothing more than an instrument of fecundity, and
destroys the whole character of that right to privacy
which is the foundation of harmonious sexual relationship.

I argue, therefore, that voluntary bodies are entitled
outside the realm where their ideas and conduct are

intended directly to alter the law, or to arrest the
continuity of general social habits, to believe what they
please and to practise what they please. This would
not permit a body of burglars to take over from Proudhon
the principle that property is theft and assume their
right to restore it to themselves; but it would justify,
to take the case of principles I personally abhor, a
society of Mormons practising polygamy in a society
like that of the United States. Let me turn from this
to the political field. I take first the question of the
right of the State to control freedom of association
in the industrial sphere. Practically speaking, the
question reduces itself to one of whether the State is
justified in limiting the power of a trade union, or of
a combination of trade unions to call out its members
on strike. I want to put on one side the technical juristic
questions involved and to discover, if I can, the justice
of the general principles which underlie the problem.

These are, I think, broadly four in number. It is
argued that the State has a right to prohibit a general
strike on the ground that this is an attempt to coerce
the government either directly, by making it introduce
legislation which it would not otherwise do, or indirectly,
by inflicting such hardship on the community that public
opinion forces the government to act. It is said, secondly,
that the State is entitled to prohibit those whom it
directly employs, for example postmen, from either
going on strike, or affiliating themselves with any
organization the nature of which may compromise the
neutrality of the government. It is said, thirdly, that
certain industries, railways, for example, or electricity
supply, are so vital to the community that continuity
of service in them is the law of their being, and that,
therefore, the right to strike can be legitimately denied
to those engaged in them. It is argued, fourthly, that
a limitation upon the purposes of trade unions, so that

they are confined within their proper industrial sphere, is also justified.

I want to analyse each of these principles separately, but certain preliminary observations are important. In any industrial society, as Mr. Justice Holmes has insisted,[1] liberty of contract always begins where equality of bargaining power begins. Granted, therefore, the normal conditions of modern enterprise, only the existence of strong trade unions will ensure to the average worker just terms in his contract of service. If he stands alone, he has neither the knowledge nor the power to secure for himself proper protection. Nor is this all. Strong trade unionism always means that public opinion can be made effective in an industrial dispute. One has only to compare the situation in the British textile industries, where the power of the unions necessarily involves a search by the State, if there is a dispute, for the terms of a just settlement, with that in America where, from the weakness of the unions, the State seems hardly to know when a dispute has occurred, where, also, the police-power is almost invariably exerted on the side of the employer, to realize the meaning of strong trade unionism. It is, in fact, the condition of industrial justice. No limitation upon freedom to associate is, I urge, permissible unless it can be demonstrated that clear and decisive advantage to the community, including, be it remembered, trade unionists themselves, is likely to result.

In this background, let us examine the first of the four principles I have enumerated. No coercion of the government, direct or indirect, is legitimate. If men want to obtain from government a solution other than government is willing to attempt, the way to that end is not by the use of industrial power, but through the ballot-box at a general election. Or, from the angle

[1] *Coppage* v. *Kansas*, 236 U.S. 1.

of indirect coercion, the first interest of the State is in the general well-being of the community; a general strike necessarily aims at that well-being and may therefore be prohibited. The general strike, even a large sympathetic strike, is in fact a revolutionary weapon. As such, it is a threat to the Constitution and illegal as well as unjustifiable.

I do not think the problem is so straightforward as the delusive simplicity of this argument would seem to make it. If it is said that the Trades Union Congress of Great Britain would not be justified in calling a general strike to compel the government to make Great Britain a federation, I should agree at once. But I point out that no one supposes it would take such action and that therefore a prohibition of it is unnecessary. But I should not agree that a general strike is unjustified to secure the eight-hour day, or to protect the payment of unemployment relief, or to continue the Trade Board system in sweated industries. Whether a general strike for these, or similar ends, would be wise is another matter. That it cannot in any circumstances be justified I am not prepared to say until I know the circumstances of some given case. I am not willing, for instance, to condemn the General Strike of 1926; on a careful analysis of its history, I believe that the blame for its inception lies wholly at the door of the Baldwin Government. No one acquainted with the character of the trade union movement but knows that a weapon so tremendous as the general strike will only be called into play on the supreme occasion. To lay it down as law that, whatever the occasion, the weapon shall not be used, seems to me an unjustifiable interference with freedom.

I am not greatly moved by the argument that it involves coercion of the government. There are occasions when that coercion is necessary, and even essential.

I believe that was the case in Great Britain in 1926. The trade unions would never have called the strike had they seen in the policy of the government even the fragment of a genuine search for justice. But the fact was that Mr. Baldwin and his colleagues simply acted as the mouthpiece of the coalowners. To illegalize a general strike in that background is to say that the trade unions should have acquiesced in the defeat of the miners without an attempt to prove their solidarity with them. It would be to announce to government that the ultimate weapon of Labour is one the use of which it need never fear. There is no danger that the general strike will ever be other than a weapon of last resort; the occasions when it can be successfully used will be of the utmost rarity. But they may occur. I cannot accept the position that government is always entitled to count on industrial peace, whatever its policy. Nor do I see why it is unconstitutional for Labour, as in 1926, to withdraw from work in an orderly and coherent way.

I do not deny, of course, that both a general strike, and others of far less amplitude, inflict grave injury and hardship upon the community. But when trade unions seek for what they regard as justice, one of their most powerful sources of strength is the awakening of the slow and inert public to a sense of the position. Effectively to do this, in a real world, it must inconvenience the public; that awkward giant has no sense of its obligations until it is made uncomfortable. When it is aroused, if, for instance, trains do not run, or coal is not mined, the public begins to have interest in the position, to call for action. Without some alternative which attempts to secure attention for a just result —I know of no such alternative—the infliction of hardship on the community seems to me the sole way, even if an unfortunate way, to the end the trade unions have in view. To limit the right to strike is a form of industrial servitude. It means, ultimately, that the worker must labour on the employer's terms lest the public be inconvenienced. I can see no justice in such a denial of freedom.

Two further points it is worth while to make. It is sometimes agreed that while the State ought not to restrict freedom of association for industrial ends, it is justified in doing so when the strike-weapon is used for some political purpose. This, indeed, was one of the objects of the Baldwin Government in enacting the Trades Disputes Act of 1927. But I know of no formula whereby such a division of purposes can be successfully made. There is no hard and fast line between industrial action and political action. There is no hard and fast line which enables us to say, for instance, that pressure for a Factory Act is industrial action, but pressure for the ratification of the Washington Hours Convention political. Extreme cases are easy to define; but there is a vast middle ground with which the trade unions must concern themselves and this escapes definition of a kind that will not hamper the trade union in legitimate activity vital to its purpose. And there are certain types of political action by trade unions—a strike against war, for example—which I do not think they ought in the interest of the community itself, to abandon. Quite frankly, I should have liked to see a general strike proclaimed against the outbreak of war in 1914; and I conceive the power to act in that way as a necessary and wise protection of a people against a government which proposes such adventures. You cannot compartmentalize life; and where grave emergencies arise, the weapons to be utilized must be fitted to meet them. A government which knew that its declaration of war was, where it intended aggressive action, likely to involve a general strike, would be far less likely to think in

E

belligerent terms. I do not see why such a weapon should be struck from the community's hand. I do not forget that the German Republic was saved from the Kapp Putsch by a general strike.

Nor must we forget the limits within which effective legal action is possible. *Jus est quod jussum est* is a maxim the validity of which is singularly unimpressive. When the issue in dispute seems to the trade unions so vital that only by a general strike can they defend their position adequately, they will, in those circumstances, defend their position whatever the law may be. Legal prohibition will merely exacerbate the dispute. It will transfer the discussion of the real problem at issue to a discussion of legality which serves merely to conceal it. A legal command is, after all, a mere static form of words; what gives it appropriateness is its relevance as just to the situation to which it is applied. And its relevance as just is made not by those who announce that it is to be applied, but by those who receive its application. The secret of avoiding general strikes does not lie in their prohibition but in the achievement of the conditions which render them unnecessary.

Nor is the denial of the right to declare a general strike a necessary protection of the total interest of the community. Right and wrong in these matters are matters to be defined in each particular case. A government which meets the threat of a general strike is not entitled to public support merely because it meets the threat. It is no more possible to take that view than it is to say that all governments deserve support when they confront a rebellion of their subjects. Everything depends on what the general strike is for, just as everything depends on the purpose of the rebellion; and the individual trade unionist must make up his mind about the one, just as the individual citizen must make up his mind about the other. Law in this realm is, in fact, largely futile. It could not prevent a general strike by men who saw no alternative open to them; and, in that event, it would merely intensify its rigours when it came. The limitation of liberty in this realm seems to me, therefore, neither just in its purpose nor beneficent in its results.

I do not, of course, deny that freedom of action in this field is capable of being abused. That is the nature of liberty. Any body of persons who exercise power may abuse it. It is an abuse of power when an employer dismisses his workmen because he does not like their political opinions. It is an abuse of power when the owners of halls in Boston refuse to hire them to the promoters of a meeting in memory of Sacco and Vanzetti. It was an abuse of power when British naval officers connived at the attempted internment of the Belgian socialist, M. Camille Huysmans, in England. It was, I think, an abuse of power when the Universities of Oxford and Cambridge refused to admit Noncomformists as students, or Parliament to seat Mr. Bradlaugh because he was an infidel. But the trade unions are no more likely, on the historic record, to abuse their power than is Parliament itself. The latter, if it wished, has the legal competence to abolish the trade unions, to disenfranchise the working classes, to confine membership of the House of Commons to persons with an independent income. We know that Parliament is unlikely to do any of these things because omnicompetence, when gravely abused, ceases to be omnicompetent. And the same truth holds, as it seems to me, of the liberty to proclaim a general strike.

A much more difficult problem arises where the second of my four principles is concerned. A government is, I think, entitled generally to the loyal and continuous service of its employees. It is therefore entitled to make regulations which restrain their liberty of action. The army and navy and the police, in particular, occupy a special position in the State; if they were free, like ordinary citizens, to withdraw their labour as they pleased, the executive power would be in an impossible position. The government, therefore, may make suitable regulations for their control. But it is important, in the framing of these regulations, that the conditions of service should be just. To be just, two principles are, I suggest, of primary importance. They should be made and administered in conjunction with those who are affected by them; and in their application or change executive action should not be the final court of appeal. The principles which, in England, we call Whitleyism are the *quid pro quo* which government servants of this type are entitled to expect in return for the surrender of the right to strike; and Whitleyism must include the right of those servants to appeal from an executive decision to such a body as the Civil Service Division of the Industrial Court. To leave the executive sole master of the field is to invite the kind of purblind folly which resulted, in 1919, in the police strikes of Boston and London. Here, certainly, the fact that the governments concerned were the judges in their own cause made it impossible for the police to get either attention or justice without drastic action. And I draw your attention to the fact that although in each case the original strikers were defeated, their successors obtained the terms, and even more than the terms, for which they fought.

The defence forces of the State constitute a special case. When we turn to the ordinary public services, central and local, quite different considerations emerge. If you analyse Whitehall, for instance, you will find a very small body of men and women who may be regarded as concerned with the making of policy; below them is another body, perhaps two or three times as large, engaged in assembling the material out of which policy is made, and applying it in minor cases; while below these once more is a vast army of clerks engaged in routine work of a more or less mechanical kind. To this last class, it cannot, I think, be said that government emerges as an employer different in kind from what they would encounter in the ordinary labour market. General economic conditions govern their pay; in France and America, indeed, it is below, rather than above, the level obtaining elsewhere for their kind of work. All their interests go along with those engaged in similar employment outside the sphere of government activity. Their union, therefore, with persons in private firms seems to me justified in order to raise their general economic level; and I do not see the justice of prohibiting it as was done by the Baldwin Government in the Trades Disputes Act of 1927. I think, further, that they are entitled to strike, if there is no other way in which they can, as they think, secure the enforcement of their demands; though I think, also, that the executive would be justified in compelling them to exhaust the resources of a comprehensive scheme of conciliation before they went so far. The history, indeed, of most modern civil services. France being a notable exception[1] shows clearly that there is no danger of officials abusing the right to strike. But it shows also the unwisdom of leaving the government free to determine the substance of the contract of service. It is just as likely as any private employer to extract the most it can get for the least it needs to give; and it is no more fit than any other employer to be left uncontrolled in this field. The more labour conditions in government service are determined finally by an independent authority, the more reasonable they are

[1] Cf. my *Authority in the Modern State*, Chap. V.

likely to be. We must not be led away by false claims
to a special majesty born of its sovereign character
to regard the State as entitled to a peculiar and uncontrolled power over its servants. History shows that
it is just as likely as anyone else to abuse an unlimited
authority.

The civil servant is not merely an employee of government; he is also a citizen. In our own day, especially,
delicate questions have arisen as to the right of the civil
servant, or of a person engaged in the armed forces
of the State, to enjoy all the normal political privileges
of a person in private employ. Is a civil servant, for
instance, entitled to enter on a political career with the
chance, if it is interrupted, to return to his department?
Most modern States, England, for instance, Canada,
South Africa, regard political activities as beyond the
area within which a civil servant may engage; France,
on the other hand, hardly limits its officials in this way,
while Germany expressly allows its officials to engage
in politics, and some fifty civil servants are now in the
Reichstag, with the power to return to their departments
if they are defeated. Certainly there are few rights for
which the rank and file of officials press so strongly
as for this; and they regard the limitation of their political
opportunities as an invasion of civic liberty at once
unnecessary and unjustifiable.

I do not think the problem is a simple one; and I
think any solution of it must therefore be complex
in character. If a high official of the Foreign Office
in England could be elected to Parliament, spend a
term there in bitter criticism of the Foreign Secretary
and then, on defeat, return to work with the minister
whom he had sought to destroy, the latter's position
would, I think, be intolerable. There is, that is to say,
a class of civil service work the very nature and associations of which involves exclusion from political life;

and if those engaged therein desire a political career, they must terminate their connexion with the civil service. We can, of course, draw a line. I see no reason why all the industrial employees of the government, postmen, for instance, or shipwrights in a national dockyard, should not enjoy all ordinary civil rights. I see no reason, either, to expect any deleterious consequences if civil servants below what we call in England the executive class are allowed ordinary political rights, so long as a decent discretion in their exercise is observed. Those engaged in the making of policy must, in my judgment, accept a self-denying ordinance in this regard. Unless government can be assured that its chief officials are aloof from political ties, it cannot trust them; and all the considerations which create a 'spoils system' will then come into play. Since experience makes it evident that a spoils system is incompatible with either honest or efficient administration, a restriction upon the liberty of public officials is, I would argue, justified. It is an inevitable part of their contract of service from the point of view of the end that service is intended to secure.

I believe, further, that this restriction applies with special force to the Army and Navy and to the police. The State is justified, in the interest of the community, in placing an absolute embargo upon the political activities of all their members. For unless this liberty is restrained, their allegiance becomes the possession of a party and they cannot give that neutral service which is the basic principle of their existence. Anyone who remembers the attempted use of the Army in 1913–14 for Ulster, the habits of the French Army during the Dreyfus period, the peculiar relations between the German Army and the Monarchy, will easily see how vital is this abstinence. There are American cities where the relations between big business and the police mean that the authority of the latter is certain to be abused in an industrial dispute. Nothing, perhaps, illustrates more nicely the delicacy of this problem than the activities of Sir Henry Wilson[1] during the years from 1912. He was, it appears, prepared to go from a meeting of the Committee of Imperial Defence to a discussion of its plans with the leaders of the Conservative opposition; and to advise with them upon the best way of rendering some of those plans nugatory. Even during the Great War he did not cease from the cultivation of political intimacies of this kind. Nor must we forget that Sir John French, at the time the Commander-in-Chief of the British Armies in France, was ready to go behind the back of the Government he served to offer secret information to the military correspondent of a Conservative newspaper; and the result of that betrayal of confidence was the breakdown of the first Asquith Government in 1915. The proper conduct of political life is clearly impossible, if the armed forces of the State are free to take a definite part in its formation. No one would endorse the Russian principle that a soldier's quality is a function of his agreement with the political faith of the government; yet once relations are established between the politician and the Army a movement towards this principle is inevitable. Sooner or later, in this condition, the Army, like the Praetorian guard, determines the personality of the State. When that occurs, no one can hope for the enjoyment of political freedom.

I turn, in the third place, to the view that industries which have a vital impact on social life can restrain the right to strike in those engaged in them. That is a peculiarly favoured doctrine at the present time; some writers even use the analogy of the Army and Navy, and argue that the principles applicable to these have

[1] Calwell, *Life of Sir H. Wilson*, Vol. II, *passim*.

a legitimate extension to this field. Others, the eminent French jurist M. Duguit, for example, take a similar view, but upon other grounds. They argue that vital public service, transport, for instance, or electricity supply, derive their whole meaning from continuity; to allow an interruption of them is, therefore, to destroy the whole law of their being.

I am as willing, I hope, as anyone to agree that an interruption of a vital public service is undesirable, and that every possible step to minimize the possibility of its occurrence should be taken. But I do not think the denial of the right to strike obtains this end in any of them; and I do not believe that the same considerations apply to every sort of vital public service. It must, I think, make a difference whether the industry is primarily operated for private profit or no; for only in the latter case is its quality as both vital and public fully recognized. No one, surely, can examine the record of the coal industry either in England or in America and say that the motives which underlie its ownership by private interest are compatible with the view that an uninterrupted service to the community has been the first object of the owners There are several reasons of primary importance for retaining the right to strike so long as private ownership continues in this sphere. If, for instance, a steamship company proposes to send out its ship under the conditions in which the *Vestris* of ill-fated memory sailed in the spring of 1929, I think the crew would be justified in striking in the public interest. So, also, I should argue that the Seamen's Union would be justified in striking, to see to it, if it could, that every vessel putting to sea carries with it wireless equipment. Again, a body of miners might, in my judgment, justifiably strike if they believed that some part of a pit to which they were to be sent was in fact too dangerous for coal to be hewed there without an alteration of the physical conditions of mining in that particular place. I should, further, urge that a strike to secure a national agreement for uniform conditions in a particular industry as against a variety of local agreement was a justifiable enterprise if that end could not be attained in any other way.

My view, broadly, reduces itself to this. Where the vital industry is in public hands, the conditions which should operate are those which relate to government service in general; where it is in private hands, the State is, I think, justified in seeing to it that the danger of dislocation is reduced to a minimum; but it is not justified in saying that, in the event of a disagreement, the men shall always abide by the results of compulsory arbitration. For, first of all, the men will not always do so; their refusal, doubtless, will be exceptional, but there will be instances in which it will occur. The famous munitions strikes on the Clyde, and the South Wales Miners' strike, during the war show that this is the case. It is, I suggest, obvious folly to attempt legislation which cannot be enforced at the critical point of urgency. The business of the State, therefore, is not to prohibit, but to find how best to make the use of the strike the final and not the first instrument in conflict.

This, I suggest, can be accomplished in two ways. It can be done, first, by limiting the profits private ownership can make in any industry of vital importance, either absolutely so that the owners are debenture-holders merely, and not the residuary legatees of any profit made, or relatively, as in a scheme like that laid down for the gas companies of London. The State is then, I suggest, legitimately entitled to argue that a curb on the liberty of the employer to make what profit he can justifies a curb on the right to strike by postulating the conditions under which alone it can become operative. Those conditions are, I think, met

by some such instrument as the Canadian Industrial
Disputes Investigation Act. Under its terms, we should
then have, at least, enforced public inquiry into the
dispute, and the consideration by both sides, as well
as by the general opinion of the community, of a reasoned
attempt at a solution of the difficulty. We respect
freedom of association by leaving it at liberty to insist
that the proposed solution is unjust, while we protect
the public interest in continuity of service by insisting
that the right to strike shall not operate until the resources
of conciliation have been exhausted.

I reject, therefore, M. Duguit's notion that public
interest in continuity of service is a paramount consideration which should over-rule all others; and I see no reason
to apply his vituperative adjectives [1] to those who take
a different view. It seems to me quite definitely a denial
of liberty for which no justification can be found to
say that men shall work on terms they think utterly
unjust; and the argument that, if they do not like those
terms, they can find other work, is, increasingly, without force in a community like our own. The number
of those in any society who have a genuine choice, at
any given time, of alternative occupations is notably
small. An electrician cannot suddenly become a barrister,
as the latter can suddenly become a journalist; and
if it is a matter of hundreds, or even thousands of men,
the compulsion upon them to continue in the vocation
for which they have been trained is obvious. The
community never gains, in the long run, from work
performed by men who labour under a sense of
injustice. That psychological feeling of frustration is
poisonous to a harmonious personality. As such, it is
incompatible with that search for freedom which I have
urged is a condition of happiness. I cannot, therefore,
agree that the community is entitled, on any terms, to

[1] *Le Droit Social*, Lect. III.

put its convenience first, and the workers' freedom afterwards.

A final problem in this same realm remains. The trade union, it is said, must obviously concern itself with all that touches the industrial conditions of its members. But it is not entitled to a general licence to roam all over the field of public activity. We should resent it if a football club passed resolutions upon the foreign policy of a government; and it is in the same way illegitimate for a trade union to deal with matters outside its sphere. The State, therefore, is entitled to define that sphere and to limit the activities of trade unions to matters that come within it.

But I have already sought to show that such a definition of spheres is, in fact, impossible of achievement. Take, for instance, foreign policy. You cannot say that trade unions ought not to concern themselves with foreign policy since this is intimately bound up with economic policy which, in turn, is the chief factor in the determination of the conditions of employment. You cannot exclude any part of the economic realm from the trade union sphere. I should agree that a trade union ought not to concern itself, let us say, with the question of whether the Pope was justified in making the Immaculate Conception a dogma of the Roman Church; but the likelihood of a trade union acting in this way is as small as that of a football club concerning itself with foreign policy. We cannot legislate for the exceptional instance. Law can only deal with normal habits susceptible of logical reduction to well-established categories. When it goes further, it merely reveals its own impotence. A trade union, moreover, is a living body; and no law has ever been successful in coping with the growth of living things by legal promulgations upon the fact of growth. Many matters are regarded today as normally and naturally within the sphere of the trade unions which

a generation ago, even a decade ago, most men would
have insisted were in nowise their concern. Let me only
remind you that in the American garment trade, the
union concerns itself, as a vital part of its function,
with the efficiency of the employers for whom its members
work. A generation ago, this would have been dismissed as
'an insolent interference with the rights of management';
today it is obvious that upon no other terms can the
function of the trade union be fulfilled. In 1914 the
unions would never have deemed it their business to
concern themselves with the bank rate and credit policy;
today they realize that these matters lie at the heart of
their problems. Any such Procrustes' bed of definition
as this principle suggests seems to me, therefore, a quite
wanton and foolish interference with freedom.

V

Such a discussion of the relation of trade unionism
to the state, illustrates, I think, the general problem
of the approach to freedom of association in the political
sphere. I have denied the right of the state to control
the internal life of such bodies; and I have sought to
show the limits of liberty where that life has rami-
fications outside their membership. It is, I think, a good
general rule that the state should not interfere in this
realm unless it must. Whenever, for example, it has
interfered with the claims of churches to lead their own
life, conflict has been the inevitable outcome. For in
any meeting of church and State, the latter will assert
its paramountcy; and a church has no alternative but
to deny that assertion. For this reason I believe that
any attempt at partnership between them is bound to
result in injury to freedom somewhere. If, as in England,
the Church is formally established by the State, its
dependency becomes obvious as soon as it develops
ideas of which the state does not approve; in matters

like marriage and divorce and education, the Church
has had to surrender positions held for centuries to
preserve the privileges of establishment. It now appears
that where there is disagreement in an established church,
the minority, on defeat, will not hesitate to go beyond
the organs which formally record the voice of the
church, in order to maintain doctrine or ritual which
the church itself seeks to change; and a legislative
assembly most members of which are either alien from
the church, or without competence in its technical
problems, will find themselves defining its most sacred
principles. Such a church, quite obviously, is the mere
creature of the state; it sacrifices its spiritual birthright
for a material mess of pottage. Or, as in the concordat
between Italy and the Papacy, there may be a looser
alliance of which the result is to deprive all non-Catholics
of their right to a secular state treating all religions
equally, in the realm of marriage and education. I
cannot avoid the conclusion that in this historic realm
only the American principle of complete separation
and non-interference can produce freedom. Unless
State and church pursue an independent path, liberty
is sacrificed; for either fusion or partnership will, in
fact, involve a conflict for supremacy.

The remaining question I wish to discuss in this
context is the right of the State over associations the
purpose of which is the overthrow of the existing
social order. What powers here ought the State to
possess? At what point can it interfere? Has it what
may be termed a preventive capacity, a right to prevent
the development of associations the natural tendency
of which will be an attempt at such overthrow? Or
should its jurisdiction be limited to punishment for
overt acts? Obviously the quality of liberty depends
very largely upon the powers we give the state in this
realm. I take it as elementary that the State has a right

to protect itself from attack. It must, as a State, assume that its life is worth preserving. It must demand that changes in its organization be the outcome of peaceful persuasion and not the consequence of violent assault. A State must, therefore, assume that its duty to maintain peace and security lies at the very root of its existence. The liberty which associations enjoy must therefore be set in the context that they cannot have a liberty to overthrow the State. To that extent, any denial of freedom to them is justified.

But what are the limits within which that denial must work? The world today is littered with organizations that are denied a legal existence and suppressed at any opportunity. The existence of a Communist party is denied by Lithuanian law; the Peasants' Party in Jugoslavia was formally dissolved; Russian principle seems to be imprisonment or exile of members of any organization which can be suspected of counter-revolutionary tendencies. We must, I think, begin with the principle that a government is not entitled to suppress associations the beliefs of which alone are subversive of the established order. For, otherwise, persecution will be built, not on fact, but on suspicion that facts may one day emerge, not on overt acts, but on principles of faith which are in truth only dangerous when they are expressed in practice. A society might be formed, for instance, to discuss and propagate the principles of Tolstoyan anarchy; I do not think any government has legitimate ground for interference with it. The time for that interference comes only when, outside the specific categories of peaceful persuasion, men have moved to action which cannot logically be interpreted as other than a determination to overthrow the social order.

I agree, for instance, that a society of Communists which began to teach its members military drill could legitimately be regarded as a direct threat to peace. So, also, when a political party, the Ulster Volunteers, for instance, or their opponents, the Nationalists, begin to purchase munitions of war, interference by government is justified. But I cannot see that a government is entitled to prevent a society of Communists from preaching their doctrines either by speech or by publication of the printed word. It is, I think, essential that, as with the English law of treason, the government should be compelled to prove the commission of some overt act which directly tends to imminent rebellion in a court of law, and to bring two witnesses at least to bear testimony to its commission. It ought not to be sufficient for a government to say that since a particular party has beliefs which include the right to violence and has elsewhere practised violence, that its suppression is legitimate. Recently, again, Mr. Ghandi announced that if the British Government did not grant Dominion Home Rule in India by the end of 1929, he and his followers would practise civil disobedience such as a refusal to pay taxes. I do not think that announcement would have justified the British Government in imprisoning Mr. Ghandi before the end of 1929 in order that he might be prevented from accomplishing his threat at a later time. Or, once more, Lord Ponsonby's organization of men pledged to refuse military service in the event of Great Britain going again to war ought not to be suppressed because, if Great Britain did go to war, some hundred thousand individuals would refuse to obey any military service Act that would then be enacted.

I am anxious, as you will see, to make it difficult for the government of a state to attack an organization the views of which it happens to dislike. In the light of the evidence, we can rest assured that, unless we compel proof, in an ordinary court of law, that overt acts have been committed, such attacks will be made. One has only to remember the Treason Trials of 1794, where there was not a scintilla of evidence against any one of the accused, or the follies enacted by governments during the Great War, to see that this is the case. In August of 1929, an Italian official actually drew public attention to the undue circulation, as he deemed, of books by Chekov, Turgenev and Tolstoy;[1] we can be sure that if a Society for the study of Russian literature had then existed in Italy, the attention of the government to its suppression would have been called. In the opening stages of the Communist trial in Meerut, the counsel for the prosecution drew attention not merely to the alleged offences of the accused, but also to the actions of the Russian Communist leaders from 1917–20, though it is difficult to see how either Indian or English Communists could have been held responsible for them. The logic, indeed, of habitual government suppression seems to be that abnormal opinion is always dangerous because, if it is acted upon, the supremacy of the law will be endangered. That is, of course, perfectly true. If the Communist Party in England sought to initiate a rebellion, there would be a threat to the supremacy of the law. But no one of common sense believes today in a Communist menace in England, least of all, perhaps, the Communists themselves. What can possibly be gained by an attempt to suppress that philosophy by an imprisonment of its members is quite beyond my understanding. I see no evidence to suggest that the slightest good has been accomplished in America by all the legislation against criminal syndicalism. Nor can I see that anything would have been gained by the kind of prohibitions which the Lusk Committee, of dubious memory, sought to put upon the statute-book.

[1] *The Observer*, 18 August 1929.

My point is that men are always entitled to form voluntary associations for the expression of grievance, and for the propagation of ideas which, as they think, will remedy what they believe to be wrong. They are not entitled to move to the commission of acts which bring them into conflict with the state. By acts I mean things like the planning of Mussolini's march on Rome, or the training of civilians as soldiers by the Ulster Defence Council. Things like these the government may legitimately attack because they have a clear and direct relation to immediate violence, actual or prospective. But governments would do well to remember, what they are too prone to forget, that they do not remove grievance, however ill-conceived, by suppressing it. And if they are allowed to associate violent opinion with actual violence, there are few follies upon which they cannot be persuaded to embark. The persecution of opinion grows by what it feeds on. Every social order is ardently upheld by fanatics who are eager to make dissent from their view a crime. The last thing that is desirable is to give them an opportunity for the exercise of their fanaticism.

It is, further, of great importance that all trials relating to these offences should be held in the ordinary courts under the ordinary forms of law. Experience makes it painfully clear that special tribunals are simply special methods for securing a conviction. For the mere creation of a special tribunal persuades the ordinary man that there is an *a priori* case against the accused, that the burden of proof lies upon him rather than upon the government. Whatever we can do to safeguard these trials from the introduction of passion is an obligation we owe to liberty. However wrong or unwise we may think the actions of men so accused, we have to remember that they represent, as a general rule, the expression of a deep-felt resentment against

social injustice. We have to protect ourselves from
protest which seeks deliberately to dissolve the bonds
of order. But it is our duty, too, to respect that protest
when it is sincerely made. And we cannot, therefore,
permit attack upon it because it represents ideas or
experience alien from our own. *De nobis fabula narretur*
is a maxim which every citizen should recognize as the
real lesson of political punishment.

Implied in all this is a view of the place of voluntary
associations in the community the significance of which
I do not wish to minimize. I am, in fact, denying that
they owe their existence to the State, or that the latter
is entitled, by means of its agents, to prescribe the
terms upon which they can live. The special place of
the State in the great society does not, in my judgment,
give it an unlimited right to effect that co-ordination
which is its function on any terms it pleases. The
principles of a legitimate co-ordination bind the State
as much as they bind any other body of men. Each of
us finds himself part of a vast organization in the midst
of which we must seek the realization of desire. We
cannot attain it alone. We have to find others with
kindred desires who will join hands with us to proclaim the urgency of their realization. There is no
other way to the attainment of that end; and an attitude,
therefore, like that of Rousseau, who denied the legitimacy of any voluntary associations, fails altogether to
take account of the elementary facts of social life.
Such bodies, indeed, must run in the leading-strings of
principle, but the question of what that principle must
be is not one the State alone is entitled to make. For
the latter is not justified in preventing the expression
of desire; it is justified only in preventing the realization
of desire by violent means. It must tolerate the expression of experience it hates because it is there, as a
State, to satisfy even the experience it cannot under-

stand. We must not, in fact, allow ourselves to fall
into the error of believing that opinion which is antagonistic to the State-purpose is unworthy to survive. The
State-purpose, like any other, is expressed through the
agency of men. They may misinterpret it; they may,
consciously or unconsciously, pervert it to their own
ends. To leave them free to settle the limits of free
association would be to leave them free to settle what
criticism of their work they were prepared to permit.
That is a power which could not safely be entrusted
to any body of men who have ever operated as a
government.

For consider, once more, the historic record. The
Roman suppression of Christianity was built upon the
belief that unity of religious belief is the necessary condition of citizenship; later experience shows that view
to be without any substance. What in fact emerges
from the history of religious persecution is the lesson
that the unity made by the suppression of Noncon-
formity is the unity of stagnation. That was the history
of France under the repeal of the Edict of Nantes; it
has been the history of Spain ever since the sixteenth
century; it is, indeed, the history of any community,
however rich and powerful, the rulers of which assume
that they know what constitute truth and right, what
opinions, therefore ,they are entitled to prescribe. Any
government which attacks a body organized to promote
some set of opinions which may become dangerous
to its safety may fairly be presumed to have something
to conceal. It is co-ordinating social life not to the end
of its greater fullness, but simply for the sake of co-
ordination.

But law, as I have insisted earlier, does not exist for
the sake of law. It is not entitled to obedience because
it is legal, because, that is, it proceeds from a source
of reference formally competent to enact it. Law exists

for what it does; and its rightness is made by the attitude adopted to it by those whose lives it proposes to shape. Since bodies like the Communist Party are in fact an announcement that some lives at least are shaped inadequately by the laws of a régime like our own, suppression seems to me an indefensible way of meeting that announcement. Force is never a reply to argument; and until argument itself seeks force as the expression of its principle, it is only by argument that it can justifiably be countered.

VI

I turn to a very different phase of the subject. In every society there are modes of conduct which, though not in themselves harmful, offer an easy prospect of becoming so. It is therefore assumed by many that it is the business of the State actively to discourage such conduct, even to the point, if necessary, of making its most innocuous expression illegal. No one is harmed, for instance, by a moderate indulgence in alcoholic liquor; but since drunkenness is harmful both to the individual and society, the State, it is said, is justified in prohibiting the manufacture or sale of alcoholic liquor. The same principle is urged of noxious drugs, of the use of tobacco, of gambling. Sometimes, indeed, the principle is carried to an extreme point and it is said that the State may prohibit any form of conduct, Sunday games, for example, which a majority of the society finds obnoxious. The claim to freedom, it is urged, may be denied in the interest of a social view of good.

I do not find it easy to accept any single principle that is obvious and straightforward as applicable to the very complex problems we encounter in this realm. Neither the fact that a mode of conduct may be harmful in excess, nor the fact that, whether harmful or no,

society dislikes it, seems to me in itself a just ground
for its suppression by the law. The first case seems
to me one for safeguards against excess; care, for instance, may be taken to see to it that it is manufactured
at a limited strength, is sold only under careful restrictions, and so on. The second case I find it impossible
to decide as a general principle, and apart from particular cases each of which is judged upon its own
merits. I am prepared, for example, to make it illegal
to keep a gaming-house; but I am not prepared to
legislate against a social game of bridge played for
money in a private house. Conduct must be punished
or prohibited when it is harmful in itself or in the
excess in which it touches society before we ought to
seek access to the clumsy machinery of the law.

For we cannot suppress all modes of conduct in which
excess does harm. In most cases, we have to leave the
individual free to judge at what point excess is a fact.
Over-eating does great harm, but no one would propose
legislation against over-eating. Many motorists sacrifice
their lives to their motor-car, especially in America;
but no one would propose legislation against an undue
indulgence in motoring. False social standards result
from our excessive adulation of film-stars and athletes;
but we should obviously be merely foolish if we legis-
lated against the publicity which makes for that excessive
adulation. We have always, I think, to study any proposed social prohibition in terms of the object to which
it is applied. We have to remember that it always runs
the risk of undermining character by a limitation of
responsibility. Men are made not by being safeguarded
against temptation but by being able to triumph over
it. It would be impossible to forbid the use of cheques
because some people succumb to the habit of embezzle-
ment. There is a clear case for forbidding the sale of
noxious drugs like heroin or cocaine except under

severe restrictions, because it is clear that in themselves
their consumption is bound to harm the recipient.
There is a clear case for insisting that persons, even if
they be passionate Christian Scientists, who are suffering from an infectious disease like small-pox, shall be
isolated until they are cured; for anyone who goes
about with small-pox inflicts direct and measurable
injury on other persons. But unless we can show that
the particular mode of conduct it is proposed to repress
must necessarily destroy the will-power of those who
practise it, as is true of noxious drugs, or directly and
unquestionably injures the rest of society in a measurable way, I think the method of prohibition an unwar-
ranted interference with freedom.

I take this view on three grounds. I believe, first,
that it is socially most important to leave the individual
as uninhibited as possible in forming his own way of
life, granted, of course, that he is adult and mature.
To shelter him at every point from experience which,
if carried to excess, may harm him is not only impossible, but also dangerous. It makes him pass his life
under the aegis of a system of fear-sanctions which,
for the most part, he will be quite unable to sublimate,
and the result will be that sense of continuous frustration which is fatal to freedom. I must, in general, learn
my own limitations by experimentation with myself.
I cannot pass my life adjusting my conduct to standards
and habits which represent the experiments of other
people. For the reasons which make the results of particular experiments seem to them convincing, I may in
my own case regard as completely unsuccessful. To
insist that their rule of life is to be mine is, normally,
to destroy my personality. It is to compel me to live
at the behest of others even where I can discover no
ground for the behest. Most people would agree that
a statute compelling an atheist to go to church was

utterly foolish. His absence does not affect the salvation of any other person. His presence there does him no good because his mood is inevitably one of gnawing indignation at being compelled to participate in ceremonies that have no meaning for him. Either he will invent excuses which enable him to stay away, or he will adopt an aggressive disbelief which makes him a source of offence to the faithful. He loses, that is, the habit of truth, on the one hand, or the capacity to give and take which makes for decent citizenship, on the other. Both forms of behaviour do real injury to him; neither produces an attitude of conviction. From the angle of character, the only rules of conduct in this realm that work, are those that are self-imposed. And these, so far as I know, are the invariable outcome of experiment made by oneself with one's own personality.

My second reason is not less important. The power of law to define modes of social conduct depends very largely upon its ability to command a sentiment of general approval. What it seeks to do must broadly commend itself, on rational grounds, to those over whose lives its principles are to preside. Legislation which does not fulfil this condition is always unsuccessful, and always has the result of bringing the idea of law itself into contempt. For where a particular statute is regarded as foolish or obnoxious by a considerable body of persons, they will rejoice in breaking it. Illegal conduct becomes a matter even of pride. It becomes a principle of conduct which gives rise to special pleasure and peculiarly satisfies human vanity. No one in London, so far as I know, regards the average policeman as an unwarrantable attack on liberty; but it seems to be the case that thousands of people in New York regard the prohibition agent in that way. They wear a breach of the law as a badge of courage, like the revolutionary in Tsarist Russia or the suffra-

gette in pre-war England; and the imposition of penalties
upon them arouses in them and their friends a sense of
angry injustice. Now I think it is an elementary principle of penal psychology that you cannot make a crime
of conduct which people do not *a priori* regard as
criminal. Popular sentiment approves a law against
murder, and you can enforce that law. But popular
sentiment, in England at least, would not, in my judgment, approve a law forbidding the manufacture and
sale of alcoholic liquor; and its chief result would be
to direct the minds of thousands to the problem of
ways and means of evading the law. That is a habit
which grows upon those who indulge in it. It loosens
all the principles of conduct which make for social
peace by making us think of the rules under which we
live as unjustifiable and oppressive. It forces social
effort quite unduly and unwisely in one direction. It
persuades it to think out mean and petty expedients
for the enforcement of the law in the same way as its
subjects think out mean and petty expedients for its
evasion. The spectacle, for instance, of the Supreme
Court deciding that the American government is entitled to tap telephone wires in order to obtain evidence
of infraction of the Volstead Act is not an encouraging
one.[1] That way lie corruption and blackmail, the kinds
of habits which, in England, we associate with names
like that of Oliver the spy,[2] in Russia with that of
agents-provocateurs like Azeff. Few things are more
detrimental than this to the moral equilibrium of a
social order.

Nor must we forget two other effects of attempted
enforcement, both of which are, I think, entirely evil.
A government which is continually flouted in its attempt at administration is bound to attempt even

[1] 277 U.S. 438.
[2] Hammond, *The Skilled Labourer*, Chap. XII.

greater severity. There will be an extension not only
of the area of offence, but also of the methods of coping
with offence, and the punishment to be inflicted where
it occurs. The classic instance of this result is the
government of Geneva from the period of Calvin's
dispensation. It does not result in the satisfactory
enforcement of the law, but in its wider evasion.
Severity on one side is met by brutality upon another;
one might as well be hanged for a sheep as a lamb.
And the disproportion between crime and punishment
which emerges draws the sympathy of the general population away from the government to the offender. This
is, I suggest, wholly bad for any society. It makes the
habits of government generally suspect to the multitude.
It creates martyrs unduly and unwisely. And this has,
of course, the consequence that it becomes ever more
impossible to enforce the law. Its irrationalism is
advertised to the multitude. It becomes inacceptable to an
ever-increasing circle who, while they may sympathize
with its principle, are not prepared to acquiesce in the
price that has to be paid for its application. Not only,
sooner or later, does such legislation perish, but the habits
to which it gives rise persist, and are frequently carried
over into realms where they are still more undesirable.
And the severity which a government is tempted to
practise makes it blind to wrong through becoming
inured to its consequences. When the British Government first met the weapon of the hunger-strike it was
baffled; later, it turned that weapon against those who
employed it by what was called the Cat and Mouse
Act. Much of this proceeding, where the suffragettes
were concerned, had a comic, as well as a tragic side.
But the whole procedure had the serious result of
making the public expect that any hunger-strike would
be a dramatic battle between the government and its
prisoner, in which the cause of the imprisonment was

lost sight of in the gamble of the procedure. The public, accordingly, was not greatly moved by the hunger-striking which took place during the Irish Revolution; and when Mr. Lloyd George left the Lord Mayor of Cork to die, people were more interested in the circumstance of his death than in the vital question of whether he should have been allowed to die. In all this realm, the denial of liberty seems to result in the slow maximization of unhappiness.

The second effect is also wholly bad. Whenever government interferes to suppress some service which a considerable body of persons think they require, when, also, the suppression is disapproved by a large number of citizens, an industry to supply that service will come into existence. Its ways will be devious, its charges will be high. It will attract to its ranks many of the most undesirable elements in society. It will form an army of lawbreakers whose habits are only too often condoned by a large section of public opinion. That has been the case with bootleggers in America and with night-clubs in London. And the risks being great, the profits are high, the interests, consequently, to be protected are correspondingly great. The history of these adventures in England and America is one of organized immorality and corruption. Condemnation by the law seems to have little or no effect in dispelling its influence. Men and women attain power through its means who normally would be shunned by most decent-minded persons. The degree to which the police are corrupted by these influences is very difficult to exaggerate. There is hardly a bribe too high for them to pay. They are organizing, too, an adventure which stimulates every sort of dubious instinct in perfectly ordinary people. Mr. Babbitt approaches his bootlegger, you will remember, in something like a religious frame of mind. The night-club *habitué* finds nothing quite so exciting as the prospect of a raid; and he leaves his meretricious surroundings with the sense that he knows the glory of danger and has escaped the humdrum pettiness of suburbia. I think it bad for society to make illegal conduct heroic. I think it still worse to make the central figures in the drama of illegality powerful in the lives of those to whom they purvey their service; men and women whose methods of obtaining a living it does not occur to their clients to condemn. Nor is it an answer to say that when the law does act, those clients immediately desert the arrested offender, which is proof that they really disapprove. An enforcement which induces cowardice at the critical moment in those who are *participes criminis* does not seem to me anything of which to be proud.

My third reason is rather different in character. Every State contains fussy and pedantic moralists who seek to use its machinery to insist that their habits shall become the official standard of conduct in the population. They are interested in prohibition and uniformity for their own sake, and every success that they win only spurs them to greater efforts. If they stop the sale of alcohol, they become ardent for the limitation of the right to tobacco. They are anxious to control the publication of books, the production of plays, women's dress, the laws governing sexual life, the use of leisure. They are terrified by what they call immorality, by which they mean behaviour of which they do not happen to approve. They are scandalized by the unconventional. They luxuriate in its denunciation. They form committees and leagues to prove the degeneracy of our times. They rush to the legislature to compel action every time they discover some exceptional incident of dubious conduct. To themselves, of course, they appear as little Calvins saving the modern Geneva from the insidious invasion of the Devil. No one, I

suppose, can seriously doubt that men like Mr. Corn-
stock regard themselves as the saviours of society.
They have an unlimited sense of a divinely appointed
mission, and the whole of their life is set in its perspective. They are the men who find in *Candide* the
means of corrupting the mind of the community. They
are horrified by the nude in art. They think the performance of *Mrs. Warren's Profession* the public
profanation of the ideal. They regard Darwin as an
'infidel' whose works were an outrage upon God; and
the circumstances of Maxim Gorky's married life seem
to them to demand his public excoriation.

I know nothing more incompatible with the climate
of mental freedom than the inference of such people.
They lack altogether a respect for the dignity of human
personality. They are utterly unable to see that people
who live differently think differently and that in so
various a civilization as ours absolute standards in
these matters are out of place. It is difficult to over-
estimate the price we pay for their successes. Certainly
no great art and no literature great in anything save
indignation can be produced where they have sway.
It is not for nothing that from the time of Calvin not
a single work of ultimate literary significance was produced by a resident of Geneva. It is easy to understand
why the grim excesses of Puritanism produced the
luxuriant licence of the Restoration. These would be,
if they could, modern Inquisitors, without tolerance and
without pity, thinking no means unjustified if only their
end can be attained. They are the kind of people who
drove Byron and Shelley into exile, and they remain
unable to see upon whom that exile reflects. Their
pride is inordinate; and human instincts are its chief
victim. They are often ignorant, usually dangerous, and
invariably active. Since the friends of liberty too often
sleep, their unceasing vigilance not seldom meets with

its reward. To me, at least, they commit the ultimate blasphemy since they seek to fashion man in their own image.

I do sincerely plead that, especially in a democratic society, these are grave dangers to ·freedom, against which we cannot too stringently be upon our guard. Especially, I say, in a democratic society. For there, the proportion of men zealous in the service of freedom, is likely to be small unless great and dramatic issues are at stake. Tyranny flows easily from the accumulation of petty restrictions. It is important that each should have to prove its undeniable social necessity before it is admitted within the fabric of the law. No conduct should be inhibited unless it can be definitely shown that its practice in a reasonable way can have no other result than to stunt the development of personality. No opportunity should be offered for the exercise of power unless by its application men are released from trammels of which it is the necessary price of purchase. We ought not to accept the easy gospel that liberty must prove that it is not licence. We ought rather to be critical of every proposal that asks for a surrender of liberty. Its enemies, we must remember, never admit that they are concerned to attack it; they always base their defence of their purpose upon other grounds. But I could not, for myself, serve principles which claimed to be just if their result was to make the temple of freedom a prison for the impulses of men.

It is because opinion is so vitally dependent upon the truthfulness of facts that observers have come more and more to insist on the connexion between liberty and the news.[1] For a judging public is unfree if it has to judge not between competing theories of what an agreed set of facts mean, but between competing distortions of what is, at the outset, unedifying and invented mythology. Things like the incident of the [M]aine, the Pekin Massacre which never occurred, the [Z]oviev letter, make an enormous difference to what Lippmann has happily termed my 'stereotype' of [en]vironment about which I have to make up my [mind]. I bring already to its interpretation a mass of [co]nceptions which tend to distort it. If there is [offe]red for me 'evidence' which has been distilled [throug]h the filter of a special interest the distortion [may be]come so complete as to make a rational judg[ment im]possible. The English journalist who invented [the] 'dole' has built into the minds of innumerable [o]f the comfortable classes a picture of the un[employed] in England as a mass of work-shy persons, [probab]ly lazy and anxious at all costs to live para[sitically up]on the taxpayer; the proven fact that less [than a frac]tion of one per cent really avoids the effort [is] unable to penetrate the miasma of tha[t]. The newspapers which belong to the Powe[r in] [A]merica, the subsidized press in Paris, th[e] [wh]ich must satisfy Mussolini or suffer su[ppression] [th]e government newspapers of Commun[ist Russia] are all efforts to dictate an environme[nt] in order that the stereotype he forms m[ay] [in]terest their owners, or controllers, [they] [pro]mote. Men may actually go out to [die for things] which they profoundly believe, tho[ugh]

[Lipp]mann's excellent analysis in *Liberty and* [the News]

CHAPTER III

LIBERTY AND SOCIAL POWER

I

LET me remind you of the essence of my argument. I have taken the view that liberty means that there is no restraint upon those conditions which, in modern civilization, are the necessary guarantees of individual happiness. There is no liberty without freedom of speech. There is no liberty if special privilege restricts the franchise to a portion of the community. There is no liberty if a dominant opinion can control the social habits of the rest without persuading the latter that there are reasonable grounds for the control. For, as I have argued, since each man's experience is ultimately unique, he alone can fully appreciate its significance himself; he can never be free save as he is able to act upon his own private sense of that interpretation. Unfreedom means to him a denial of his experience, a refusal on the part of organized society to satisfy what he cannot help taking to be the lesson of his life.

But no man, of course, stands alone. He lives with others and in others. His liberty, therefore, is never absolute, since the conflict of experience means the imposition of certain ways of behaviour upon all of us lest conflict destroy peace. That imposition, broadly speaking, is essential to liberty since it makes for peace; and peace is the condition of continuity of liberty. The prohibitions, therefore, that are imposed are an attempt to extract from the experience of society certain principles of action by which, in their own interest, men ought to be bound. We cannot, indeed, say that all the principles a given government imposes are those it ought to impose. We can only say that some principles, by being imposed, are bound up with the very heart of freedom.

That is the paradox of self-government. Certain restraints upon freedom add to a man's happiness. Partly, they save him from the difficulty of going back to first principles for every step he has to take; they summarize for him the past experience of the community. Partly, also, they prevent every opposition of desire from resulting in conflict; they thus assure him of security. In a sense, he is like a traveller who reaches a sign-post pointing in many directions. Law helps him by telling him where one, at least, will lead; and it invites him to assume that its direction is also, or should be, his destination. Clearly this will not always be the case. For it to be so, the end of the law must be his as well, its experience must not contradict his own. For that contradiction, as a rule, means punishment for him since, at the end of the road he takes, if it is not the path of the law, he will find a policeman waiting for him. We must, that is to say, find ways of maximizing our agreement with the law.

I sought earlier to show that this maximization can only take place when the substance of law is continuously woven from the fabric of a wide consent. Here I propose to inquire into certain essential conditions which determine whether that consent can be obtained. I propose to inquire, in other words, into that weird complex of prejudice, judgment, interest, which we call public opinion and to seek the terms of its adequate relationship to liberty. For if my argument be valid that a man's citizenship is the contribution of his instructed judgment to the public good, and that right action, for him, is action upon the basis of that judg-

ment, clearly, the factor of instruction is of d importance. Instructed judgment is considered a impulsive, ultimate and not immediate. It is a c sion arrived at after an attempt to penetrate b the superficial appearance to what is truth-seemin is a decision made after evidence has been collecte weighed, distortion allowed for, prejudice discounted If, for instance, I am to oppose the State in a matt like military service, I ought not to do so until I h rigorously examined the facts upon which I build principles. And, *mutatis mutandis*, that is true o aspect of social activity. The first urgency is that the facts upon which I base my action

Now the world of facts which impinge u us is difficult and complex and enormous. can know all of that world. A large pa be in some context a fundamental pa take on trust from other persons. O primary importance that the things should correspond with the reality right judgment can be made. My peace-terms that should be made w one thing if I believe that Germ crucify innocent Belgian citizen and cut off the breasts of their another thing if I believe that like other people, decent, kir much the same things in life to the nationalization of th foundly depend upon, fir industry itself, and, seco tion of nationalization i vast majority of the p my own inquiries int time, I have to halt this paper's account

the cause which, as they judge, embodies those purposes has not, in fact, the remotest connexion with it.

We have, in short, the difficulty that the control of news by special interests may make prisoners of men who believe themselves to be free. The Englishman who has to form an opinion about a miners' strike is not likely to be 'free' in any sense to which meaning can be attached if the facts which he encounters have been specially doctored in order to make it as certain as possible that he conclude in favour of the mine-owners. A Chinaman who hears that the 'Liberal' party in Rumania has won a victory at the polls, an American who is informed that London is governed by Municipal 'Reformers', approaches the discovery of the facts with a body of preconceptions, derived from quite alien experience, which will make a true judgment of those facts a very complex matter. In the Conference of The Hague upon reparations in August 1929, the Italian newspapers continued to paint Mr. Snowden as the Shylock withholding from Italy its due share, while the English Press was equally unanimous in painting him as the protagonist against a continental effort to make Great Britain the milch-cow of Europe. The Italian, or the Englishman, who wished to obtain a just view of the issues really at stake there, would have had to engage in arduous researches into technical material about which he might lack competence and for which he would certainly not easily find leisure.

Let us remember, too, that our stereotype of the contemporary environment is only the last phase, so to speak, of the problem. The psychologists are unanimous in telling us how important for our future are the impressions we gather in our early years. Clearly, from that angle, the things we are taught, the mental habits of those who teach us, are of quite primary urgency. It may make all the difference to the intel-

lectual climate of a people whether, for instance, the
history learned by children in schools is wide and
generous, or parochial and narrow, whether its teachers
cultivate the sceptical mind, or the positive mind.
People who are imprisoned in dogmas in childhood
will have an agonizing struggle to escape from its
stereotypes, and they may well have been so taught
that they either, after effor᷑ ᷑uccumb, or do not even
know that it is necess᷑
know how to emphasize
able importance to freeᷗ
educational process.

Teach a child year in and year out that the American
Constitution is the ultimate embodiment of political
wisdom and you increase tenfold the difficulty of
rational and necessary amendment by the generation
to which that child belongs. Set him under teachers
like those of whom Professor Harper tells us that
seventy-seven per cent 'contended that one should never
allow his own experience and reason to lead him in
ways that he knows are contrary to the teaching of the
Bible', and fifty-one per cent that 'our laws should
forbid much of the radical criticism that we often hear
and read concerning the injustice of our country and
government', and the openness of mind upon which
reason depends for its victories will be well-nigh unattainable.[1] Those only who realize the importance of
education will understand how a Southern audience
could go wild with anger over an account, in large
outline untrue, of German atrocities, and yet listen
with indifference to the description of a lynching in
their own community so revolting in its detail as to
be unfit almost for transcription. And we must add
to the school influence in childhood, that of the home,

[1] I take my account from a summary in the *Lantern* (Boston),
July 1929.

the church, the streets, in the terrible certainty that there are few impressions which do not leave their trace.

It is unnecessary, if I may so phrase it, to urge men to live dangerously. To the degree that their happiness depends upon making their decisions conform to the facts, they cannot avoid danger. It is dangerous to leave a child in the hands of teachers who believe that all experience and reason must be abandoned which does not square with that recorded in the partly mythical annals of a primitive Semitic tribe several thousand years ago, or who equate patriotism with a fervid acceptance of the present political system. The adult is endangering his happiness if he believes that truth is what Karl Marx said, or Mussolini tells him, or the inferences of Mr. Baldwin which the latter has in turn drawn from material prepared for him by the Research Department of the Conservative Central Office. Happiness depends upon being able to approach with an open mind facts which have been prepared by independent persons who have no interest in seeing that their incidence is bent in some particular way. Anything else imprisons the mind in dogmas which only work so long as that mind does not travel beyond the narrow confines within which the dogmas work. Once it goes beyond, unhappiness is the inevitable outcome.

How are we to get independent fact-finding and the open mind? The answer, of course, is the tragic one that there is no high road to it. Partly, it lies in the development of particular techniques, but, most largely, it lies in the kind of educational methods we use, and this, in its turn, in the purposes for which those methods are employed. I entirely agree that a multiplication of independent fact-finding agencies, as disinterested and impartial about wages and other social conditions as a medical man in the making of a diagnosis, will take us some distance.[1] Not, I think, very far; for between the finding of facts by independent agencies and the driving of them home to the public are interpolated just those factors of special interest which are the enemies we confront. I agree, too, that freedom is rarely better served than when a great public organ falls into the hands of one who, like C. P. Scott with his *Manchester Guardian*, determines to make news and

izatıon into a profession with standards of entrance and performance, will add greatly to the chances of solving the problem. So, also, will the development of specialized journals of opinion, and new inventions like the wireless. To some extent—not, I think, a great extent—competitive fact-finding makes for truth. Outrageous propaganda kills itself; men do not believe the 'papers' because they have found them lying at some point where the facts forced themselves upon attention.

And so, too, with a training for the open mind in schools. People may come to see that where the quality of intelligence is concerned, the second-rate, the dull, the incurious, the routineer, simply will not do. They may be prepared to make education a profession sufficiently well paid to attract the highest ability, and sufficiently honourable to satisfy the keenest ambition. Even now we cannot over-estimate the influence exerted in his generation by a great teacher. Do what we will, let him teach what he please, the minds with which he is in contact will go along with his mind, they will learn his enthusiasms, share his zest in inquiry. It may be Huxley in London, William James in Harvard, Alain in Paris. Students who have lived with such men

[1] Lippmann, *Public Opinion*, p. 379 f.

are their spiritual children not less than those who
have learned the habits of a gentleman at Eton or a
proper respect for the Emperor of Japan in Tokio.
And, equally, we may learn that a narrow patriotism
in history and politics has social results less admirable
than a quick scepticism built from the sense that our
country has not always been right, our institutional
standards not invariably perfect. Our governors may
be willing to admit that one inference from the rebellion
of Washington is the possible legitimacy of rebellion,
one inference even from the new theology of Jesus,
that we are sometimes justified in the making of new
theologies. It is even possible that the value of the
power to think may become so much more widely
recognized, that we shall not ask that those who are
able creatively to teach this supreme art, be dismissed
because we dislike either what they teach or the opinions
they profess outside the practice of their profession.
We may come to insist upon security of tenure for the
teacher even when his principles of faith do not coincide
with those for which we desire the triumph.

Yet these possibilities do not, in themselves, seem to
me to confer a right to optimism if they stand alone.
If it pays to spread false news, let us be sure that false
news will be spread. If some special interest gains by
corrupting the facts, so far as it can, the facts will be
corrupted. If a poor educational system strengthens
the existing foundations of power, it will tend to remain
poor; if its extension is costly, those who are to bear
the cost will find good reason either not to extend it,
or to proceed at such a snail's pace that the new way
has no chance of affecting mankind except in terms of
geological time. Our difficulty is the twofold one that
propaganda can produce immense results in a brief
space of time and that creative educational change
takes something like a generation before its results are

manifest upon a wide scale. The forces at work to
prevent the emergence of truth, the forces, also, which
have every reason to dislike the development of the
mind which seeks for truth, are many and concentrated
and powerful. They do not want the general reporting
of experience, but only of that experience which favours
themselves. They do not want the general population
so trained as to prize truth, but only so trained that
they believe whatever they read. In our own day it
would not be an unfair description of education to
define it as the art which teaches men to be deceived
by the printed word. Those who profit by that decep-
tion are, at the moment, the masters of society.

For we must remember that in these matters we
have to concern ourselves with short-term values and
not long-term values. We do not legislate for some
conceivable Utopia to be born in some unimaginable
time, but for the kind of world we know ourselves, for
lives like our own lives. The freedom we ask we have
to make. Every postponement we accept, every failure
before which we are dumb, only consolidates the forces
that are hostile to freedom. They themselves realize
this well enough. They have, in the past, fought every
step on every road to freedom because they have seen
that the accumulation of small concessions will, in the
end, be their defeat. Everywhere they have been guilty
of definite error, or wrong, they have denied the error
or wrong, lest it upset faith in their own right to power.
Not the least powerful to silence, you will recollect,
which persuaded even those who thought Sacco and
Vanzetti innocent was their fear that proof of that
innocence might disturb popular faith in the Massachusetts Courts. The same was true in the Dreyfus
case. The same, on a lesser plane, was true of Mr.
Winston Churchill when he sought to deceive the
House of Commons over the treatment of Lady Constance

Lytton in prison.[1] Those in power will always deny freedom if, thereby, they can conceal wrong. And any successful denial only makes its repetition easier. Had California released Mooney in 1916, when the world knew he was innocent, it would have been easier for Massachusetts to have acted justly ten years later. The will to freedom, like the will to power, is a habit, and it perishes of atrophy.

The inference I would draw is the quite basic one that in any society men only have an equal interest in freedom when they have an equal interest in its results. Where those results are already possessed by some, they seldom have the imagination to see the consequence of their denial to others. They will persuade themselves that those others are contented with their lot, or made differently in nature, so that they are unfit to enjoy what others possess. There is no myth we are not capable of inventing to lull our conscience. We see the futility of action on our part, because we are so unimportant. We see that it would be dangerous in this particular case, because we have an influence that, in other cases, might be exerted to useful purpose. We do not think the time has come for action. We think that action here might lead to other and quite unjustifiable demands. We would have associated ourselves with the demand, but those who are making it, or the way in which it is being made, unfortunately renders this impossible. Life is so complex and tangled and full, that those who desire to abstain from the battle for freedom can always find ample excuse. The workman may be afraid for his job; Babbitt may shrink from being shunned by the group whose fellowship is his life; it may be the handful of silver, the riband for the coat, the love of power, the loathing of what freedom may bring. Whatever the motive of abstention,

[1] Cf. Lady Constance Lytton, *Prisons and Prisoners*.

let us remember that men think differently who live differently, and that, as they think, so they build principles of action to remedy what, in their lives, they find bitter or unjust, to preserve what they find pleasant or right.

We cannot, of course, remedy all experience which makes for a sense of bitterness or injustice. Things like the betrayal of friendship are, only too often, beyond the power of organization to affect. But the sense of bitterness or injustice that comes from bad housing, low wages, or the denial of an adequate political status, these we are able to remedy by social action. Or, rather, we are free to move to their remedy, if we have an equal interest in doing so. If our interest is unequal, our sense of a need to share with others in action will be small. Other things will seem more significant or more urgent; and the need itself will shrink as it obtrudes. The less we live in the experience of our neighbours, the less shall we feel wrong in the denial of their wants. Trade unionists appreciate a demand for higher wages more keenly than employers: the wealthy rentier reads of a strike in the cotton trade as a newspaper incident, of a railway dispute, whatever its grounds, as a threat to the community. The sense of solidarity comes only when the result of joint action impinges equally on the common life.

We are in the difficulty that every step we take towards freedom is a step towards the equalization of privileges now held unequally. Those who hold them are not anxious to abandon what they entail; sometimes they can even persuade themselves that the well-being of society depends upon a refusal to surrender them. For them, therefore, the honest publication of facts, the making of free minds, are simply paths to disaster. Why should they surrender their weapons of defence? Why, the more, when many of them do not

even suspect that they fight with poisoned weapons ?
To explain to a loyal Roman Catholic that he should
tell his children that there is grave reason to deny the
truth of all he believes is to invite him to shatter the
foundation upon which he has built his life. To suggest to the average citizen who took part in the Great
War that his school-books should abandon the legend
that his particular state entered it with the whole-
souled motive of serving justice would appear scandalous
simply because he is honestly unconscious of any other
motive. To urge even upon the public-spirited heir to
a great estate the possible duty of acting upon the
principle of Mill's argument about the laws of inheritance
is, at the best, an adventure in the lesser hope. There
was good reason for the unpopularity of the Socratic
temper in Athens.

II

I conclude, therefore, that whatever our mechanisms
and institutions, liberty can hope to emerge and to be
maintained in a society where men are, broadly speaking,
equally interested in its emergence and its maintenance.
I accept the insight Harrington had when he insisted
that the distribution of economic power in a State will
control the distribution of its political power. I think
James Madison was right when he argued that property
is the only durable source of faction. I think the perception of the early socialists entirely justified when
they urged that a society divided into a small number
of rich, and a large number of poor persons, will be
a society of exploiters and exploited. I cannot believe
that, in such an atmosphere, liberty will be a matter
of serious concern to the possessors of power.

What will concern them is how they can best maintain their power. They will permit anything save the
laying of hands upon the ark of their covenant. They
will allow freedom in inessentials; but when the pith

of freedom is attack upon their monopoly they will define it as sedition or blasphemy. For if the form of social organization is a pyramid, men are bound to struggle towards its apex. In a society of economic unequals, gross unequalities make conflict inherent in its foundations. The possession of wealth means the possession of so much that makes for a happy life, beautiful physical surroundings, leisure to read and to think, safeguards against the insecurity of the morrow. It is, I think, inevitable that those to whom these things are denied should envy those who possess them. It is inevitable, also, that envy should be the nurse of hate and faction. Those who are so denied struggle to attain, those who possess struggle to preserve. Justice becomes the rule of the stronger, liberty the law which the stronger allow. The freedom that the poor desire in a society such as this is the freedom to enjoy the things their rulers enjoy. The penumbra of freedom, its purpose and its life, is the movement for equality.

And it is equality that is decried by those who rule. It means parting with the exercise of power and all the pleasures that go with its exercise. It means that their wants do not define the ends of production, their standards do not set the objects of consideration, their right to determine the equilibrium of social forces is no longer recognized. Equality, in fact, is a denial of the philosophy of life which is bred into their bones by their way of living. It does not seem to me remarkable that they should fight against this denial. Who of us, on these terms, but would find it difficult to accept as valid experience which contradicts our experiences, a system of values which attempts the transvaluation of our own? Who of us but would not feel that a freedom which seeks radical alteration of the contours of existence is perverse and dangerous and worthy only to be suppressed? The Pagan felt that of the Christian, the Catholic of the Protestant, the landowner of the merchant. The new power which seeks its place in the sun is inevitably suspected by the old with whom it claims equal rights.

The equality will be denied, and, with it, the freedom to claim equality. Inevitably, also, the right to freedom will be maintained, and the two powers will, sooner or later, mass their forces for battle. I know no instance in history in which men in possession of power have voluntarily abdicated its privileges. They say that reason and justice prevail; but they mean their reason and their justice. They are prepared to coerce in the hope of success, and they are prepared to die fighting rather than to surrender. It is the result of such a way of life that the ideal of freedom is inapplicable to matters upon which there is urgent difference of opinion between the rulers and their subjects. It is impossible for reason to prevail if men are prepared to fight about the consequences of its victory. And if they are prepared to fight there is no room in the society for freedom since this is incompatible with habits of violence.

Any society, in fact, the fruits of whose economic operations are unequally distributed will be compelled to deny freedom as the law of its being; and the same will be true of any society in process of forcible transition from one way of life to another. Cromwellian England, Revolutionary France, Communist Russia, Fascist Italy, each of these, of set purpose, made an end of the pretence that freedom was a justifiable object of desire. In each, it was proposed to maintain some particular form of social organization at any cost; to inquire into the cost might result in doubt of the value of the effort; and the value of that freedom which releases reason was therefore denied. A revolutionary State, of course, makes the position peculiarly clear. But it is not merely true of the revolutionary State.

In England, or France, or Germany, there is no freedom where the fundamentals of the society are called into question, if their rulers think that this may cause danger to those questions. The government may decide that William Godwin is innocuous; but it will not hesitate to convict Tom Paine—in truth far less drastic—of high treason. The cause of this attitude is, I think, beyond discussion. If freedom seeks to alter fundamentals, freedom must go; and freedom can hardly help but concentrate on fundamentals in a society distinguished by economic inequality. I do not need to point out to you the extraordinary timidity of society before subversive discussion of property-rights, nor to insist upon the complicated legal precautions that are taken for its defence. You have only to examine the attitude in which Labour combinations are approached by those who possess economic power, as instanced, for example, by the use of the injunction by American judges,[1] to realize that the main purpose of limitations on freedom is to prevent undue encroachments upon the existing inequalities. We announce that we are open to conviction in matters of social arrangement. But we take the most careful steps to see that our convictions are not likely to be overthrown.

For the chance that reason will prevail in an unequal society is necessarily small. It is always at a disadvantage compared with interest, for, to the latter, especially in property matters, passion is harnessed, and in the presence of passion people become blind to truth. They see what they want to see, and they select as truth that which serves the purpose they desire to see prevail. The preparation of news for the making of opinion is, indeed, extraordinarily like the old religious controversy in which men hurled text and counter-text

[1] Cf. Frankfurter and Green, *The Injunction in Labour Dispute* (1930).

at one another. The real problem was one of proportions; but the protagonists altered the proportions that
the material might the better serve their cause. Some
years ago, a Labour Delegation returned from Russia
with a statement about its character from Peter Kropot-
kin. A leading capitalist newspaper in London printed
all those parts of it which attacked the Russian régime;
and the leading Labour newspaper printed those parts
of it favourable to the Bolshevik experiment. The readers
of the first were, therefore, satisfied with the knowledge
that an eminent anarchist heartily disliked Bolshevism;
and the readers of the second were heartened by dis-
covering that so eminent a friend of freedom was nevertheless prepared to support a Dictatorship as favourable to freedom. You will remember that Luther and
Calvin were always prepared to abide by the plain
words of Scripture; but each was careful, at critical
points, to insist that his own interpretation alone
possessed validity. In that atmosphere, a solution which
strikes opposing controversialists as just is not, at
least easily, to be found.

This, I suggest, is the kind of environment any plea
for freedom must meet in the modern State. Discussion
of inessentials can be ample and luxurious; discussion
of essentials will always, where it touches the heart of
existing social arrangements, meet at least with difficulty and probably with attack. It will find it extraordinarily hard to organize supporters for its view, if
this opposes the will of those in authority. In war-time,
any plea for reasonableness is at a discount; and it
was at a discount in England during the general strike
when the government sought at once for the conditions
of a belligerent atmosphere. Attack an interest, in a
word, and you arouse passion; arouse passion, especially
where property is concerned, and the technique of *raison
d'état* will sooner or later be invoked. But liberty and

raison d'état are mutually incompatible for the simple reason that *raison d'état* is a principle which seeks, *a priori*, to exclude rational discussion from the field. It seeks neither truth nor justice, but surrender.

It is a technique, I think, which almost always comes into play when dangerous opinion is challenged by the State. A good instance of this is afforded by the trial of the British Communists in 1925. No one could seriously claim that their effort constituted a serious menace to the State, for they were a handful among millions, and there was not even evidence that their propaganda met with any success. Yet their condemnation was a foregone conclusion, granted the terms of the indictment. And the habits of power were interestingly illustrated by the judge who presided over the trial. He had conducted the case with quite scrupulous fairness, and had shown no leaning to one side or the other until the jury had rendered its verdict. He then made an offer to the defendants that if they would abandon their belief in Communism he would adjust the sentence in the light of that abandonment. He made the offer, I do not doubt, in the utmost good faith and an entirely sincere conviction that Communist opinions are morally wicked. But that attitude was precisely similar to the Roman offer to the early Christians: they could avoid the arena if they would offer but a pinch of incense on the pagan altar. It was precisely similar to the willingness of the Inquisitor to mitigate his sentence where there is confession of heresy and repentance. Mr. Justice Swift seemed to have no realization at all that the defendants were Communists in the light of an experience of social life which, for them, was as vivid and compelling as the Christian revelation to its early adherents; that the offer he made to them was mitigation of punishment in return for the sacrifice of their sincerity; that the State, for him, was Hobbes' 'mortal God' at whose altar they must do reverence. His views, of course, were the natural expression of his own experience of life, and, without doubt, sincerely held; but they implied an inability imaginatively to understand alien experience which is pathetic in the limitation it involves. And perhaps the supreme irony in the situation was the fact that to be tried as Communist was, for the defendants, perhaps the highest test of truth to which their faith could be submitted.

When Plato, in the *Laws*, set out a revised version of his ideal polity for application to the real world about him, he surrendered his demand for the complete communism which had distinguished his Utopia. But he was still emphatic enough about the need for equality to lay it down that no member of his State should possess property more than four times in amount of that owned by the poorest citizens. The ground of that drastic conclusion was quite clear in his mind. Great economic inequalities are, as he saw, incompatible with a unity of interest in the community. There is no common basis upon which citizens can move to the attainment of kindred ideals. The lives of the few are too remote from the lives of the many for disagreement about social questions to be possible in terms of peace, if the ultimate organization of the society is not to be changed. The remoteness means that the few will always fear the invasion of their privilege, and the many will envy them its possession. It is not only, as I have said, that men think differently who live differently; it is, essentially, that men think antagonistically who live so differently. That antagonism is bound to result in violence unless the domination of the many by the few is almost complete, or is tempered by so continuous a flow of concession as results, in the end, in the effective mitigation of the inequality.

There cannot, in a word, be democratic government without equality; and without democratic government there cannot be freedom.

For the real meaning of democratic government is the equal weighing of individual claims to happiness by social institutions. A society built upon economic inequality cannot attempt that sort of measure. Consciously or unconsciously, it starts from the assumption that there is a greater right in some claims than in others. It cannot be said that response to claims is made in terms of justice. The nature of economic inequality is a compulsion to respond to effective demand, and this pays no regard to science on the one hand, or to need upon the other. It thinks only of the presence of purchasing power and not of its connotation in terms of social purpose. The whole productive scheme is thereby tilted to the favour of those who possess the power to make their wants effective. There is cake for some before there is bread for all. The palace neighbours the slum. And those who find that their wants do not secure attention are, inevitably, tempted to an examination of the moral foundations of such a society. Their interest drives them to demand its reconstruction in terms of those wants. Liberty means, in such a context, the power continuously to exercise initiative in social reconstruction. The whole ethos which surrounds their effort is that of equality. They search for freedom for no other end but this.

I do not need to remind you that most observers who have sought to estimate the significance of the democratic movement have seen that equality is the key to its understanding. That was the case with Tocqueville; it was the case with John Stuart Mill; and, in a famous lecture which reads now as though it was the utterance of a prophet,[1] it was the case, also,

[1] See the lecture on Equality in *Mixed Essays*.

with Matthew Arnold. Broadly, their insight converged towards a recognition of three important things. They realized, first, that in any society where power is gravely unequal, the character and intelligence of those at the base is unnaturally depressed. The community loses by this in two ways. The energy and capacity of which it might make use are not released for action; and the concentration of effective power in a few hands means that the wishes, opinions, needs, of the majority do not receive sufficient consideration. An aristocracy, whether of birth, or creed, or wealth, always suffers from self-sufficiency. It is inaccessible to ideals which originate from without itself. It tends to think them unimportant if they are urged tactfully, and dangerous if they are urged with vigour. It is so accustomed to the idea of its own superiority, that it is resentful of considerations which inquire into the validity of that assumption. It may be generous, charitable, kind; but the surrounding principle of those qualities is always their exercise as of grace and not in justice. An aristocracy, in a word, is the prisoner of its own power, and that the most completely when men begin to question its authority. It does not know how to act wisely at the very moment when it most requires wise action.

It is not only that any aristocracy becomes unduly absorbed in the consideration of its own interests. Its depression of the people has the dangerous effect of persuading the latter of its necessary inferiority. It is unable to carry on its own affairs with order and intelligence. It does not know how to represent its wants with decision. It develops a sense of indignation because its interests are neglected; but it does not know how to attach its indignation to the right objects or, when so attached, how to remedy the ills from which it suffers. An aristocracy, in a word, deprives its subjects of character and responsibility; and as the revolutions of 1848 so clearly demonstrated, while they can destroy, they have never been taught how to create. The success of the Puritan Rebellion and the American Revolution was built upon the fact that, in each case, the exercise of power had been a habit of the general population; in the one case in the management of Nonconformist Churches, in the other in the governance of local legislatures and township meetings. In each case, a blind government confronted men who knew how to formulate their wants, and to organize their attainment. But, in general, aristocracies do not provide their subjects with this opportunity. Their own effort is substituted for popular effort, their own will for the popular will. The development of the total resources at their disposal is postponed to the preservation of their interest and convenience. They dwarf the masses that they may the better contemplate the stateliness of their own state. But that, in the end, always means that the vital power of the people is absent at the moment when it is most required.

The third weakness of aristocracies is their inevitable impermanence. There is no method known of confining character and energy and ability to their own ranks. These, where they emerge in the people, will always seek the means of their satisfaction. From this angle, few things are so significant as the history of the British Labour Party. It rose to power largely because there was no room in the leadership of the historic parties for self-made men who had not sought success either as lawyers or as business men. The result was that the knowledge at the disposal of Liberals and Conservatives, the significant experience upon which they could draw for the making of their policy, was always more narrow than the area of the problems they had to meet.

The lives of the typical Labour leaders of the second generation, Keir Hardie, Mr. Ramsay MacDonald, Mr. Arthur Henderson, invariably show a period where the regretful decision has to be taken against further co-operation with a party which cannot see the needs they see, which does not desire service to the ideals they seek to serve.[1] And men such as these make articulate in the minds of all who have a sense that their interests are neglected not only the fact of negligence, the demand, therefore, for satisfaction, but also the search for the principles whereby satisfaction can be attained. Their insight into an emphasis to which little attention has been paid grows by the volume of the experience they counter into a movement; and those who have permitted the interest to be neglected find that the old battle-cries no longer attract its allegiance even when they are given new form.

It is curious to note that not even the impact of defeat gives this lesson its proper perspective to the defeated. English Liberalism has suffered eclipse because, broadly speaking, it was unable to discover an industrial philosophy suitable to the wants of the new electorate. It served admirably the requirements of the manufacturer and the shopkeeper who were enfranchised in 1832. It gave them freedom of trade, liberty of contract and full religious toleration. But it never understood either the fact of trade unionism or the philosophy of trade unionism. Its attitude to citizenship was atomic in character. It saw the community as a government on the one side, and a mass of discrete individuals on the other. It assumed that each of these, given liberation from the special privilege of the *ancien régime*, had the full means of happiness at his disposal; it accepted, in a word, the principles of Benthamite

[1] See for instance, the very interesting letter of Mr. MacDonald to Keir Hardie in W. Stewart, *Life of Keir Hardie* (1921), p. 92.

radicalism as absolute. But its error was not to see
that the community is not merely a mass of discrete
individuals. Jones is not merely Jones, but also a
miner, a railwayman, a cotton operative, an engineer.
As one of these, he has interests to be jointly pro-
moted and jointly realized. A philosophy of politics
that is to work must find a full place in the state
for organized workers to whom freedom in the industrial
sphere is, in its fullest implications, as urgent and as
imperative as freedom in the sphere of politics or
religion.

The Liberal Party did not see this until it was too
late. Built largely on the support of the Nonconformist
business man, the interests it understood were essentially
his interests; and to recognize the implications of trade
unionism, as Keir Hardie and his colleagues did, was
to invade the interests upon which it was able to count
for allegiance. It was forced, obviously unwillingly,
into concessions like the Trades Disputes Act of 1906;
but its policy, as the detailed history of the process of
social legislation from 1906 to 1914 makes clear was,
so far as it could, to mitigate social inequality by recognition of individual claims, and to build machinery
for their satisfaction which continued to neglect the
fact of trade unionism. When, after the war, the
remarkable growth of the Labour Party showed how
vast was the decline of the Liberal hold upon the
working-classes, the Liberal leaders were driven, by the
need of self-preservation, to the invention of industrial
principles likely to prove attractive to trade unionists.
But these wore the air of being produced for the occasion; and they did not fit into the character of Liberal
Leadership. For the latter was quite unable to attract
to its ranks either working-men candidates or trade
union support; and the emphatic declaration of a
Liberal politician that his party could not join the ranks

of Labour because the latter was built upon the trade
unions showed how unreal was the body of industrial
principles which Liberalism had developed.[1] It remained
an atomic philosophy applicable to a world in which
employer and worker confronted each other, as individuals, on equal terms. The assumption was unjustified;
and the way lay open for the consolidation by Labour
of its growing hold upon the workers. Liberalism
remained a middle-class outlook, admirable in its exposition of basic principle, but incapable of adjusting
principle to a medium with which its supporters were
largely unacquainted.

In an interesting passage[2] Lord Balfour has drawn
attention to the fact that the success of the British
Constitution in the nineteenth century — it is worth
adding the general success of representative government
—was built upon an agreement between parties in the
State upon fundamental principles. There was, that is,
a kindred outlook upon large issues; and since fighting
was confined to matters of comparative detail, men
were prepared to let reason have its sway in the realm
of conflict. For it is significant that in the one realm
where depth of feeling was passionate—Irish home
rule—events moved rapidly to the test of the sword;
and the settlement made was effected by violence and
not by reason. That was the essence of the Russian
problem. The effort to transform a dull and corrupt
autocracy into a quasi-constitutional system came, like
the efforts of Louis XVI at reform, too late to affect
men who had already passed beyond any possibility
of compromise with the idea of monarchical power.
The concessions which the autocracy was prepared to
offer did not touch the fringe of what the opposition

[1] Mr. Ramsay Muir in the *Nation*, 17 August 1929.
[2] Preface to the World's Classics edition of Bagehot's *English
Constitution*, p. xxiii.

regarded as nominal. Nor was that all. Post-war
Russia illustrated admirably the truth of Mill's insistence that 'a State which dwarfs its men in order that
they may be more docile instruments in its hands, even
for beneficial purposes, will find that with small men
no great thing can really be accomplished; and that
the perfection of machinery to which it has sacrificed
everything, will in the end avail it nothing, for want
of the vital power which, in order that the machine
might work more smoothly, it has preferred to banish.'

III

I conclude, therefore, that the factor of consent is
not likely effectively to operate in any society where
there is a serious inequality of economic condition; and
I assume, further, that the absence of such consent is,
in the long run, fatal to social peace. I do not deny
that men will long postpone their protest against that
absence; there are few wrongs to which men do not
become habituated by experience, few, therefore, which,
after the long passage of time, they will not be persuaded are inherent in nature. But such habituation
is never permanent; sooner or later someone arises,
like the child in the fairy-story, to point out that in
fact the emperor is naked. If attention is drawn to
some need which is widely experienced, the denial that
the need is real by those who have not experienced it,
will not prove effective. Working-men never found it
easy to believe that long hours of work or low wages
were the essential conditions of industrial leadership in
the nineteenth century. Few Nonconformists sympa-
thized with Burke's attitude to parliamentary reform.
Few American trade unionists see in the use of the
injunction by the courts a method of preserving social
peace in terms of a strict impartiality between capital

[1] *On Liberty* (People's edition), p. 68.

and labour. Opponents of Mussolini are not moved
by his plea that he thinks only of the well-being of
Italy. Russian working-men have probably been often
tempted to the view that their Bolshevik masters mistake Communist dogma for social truth.

To satisfy experience, in short, we must weigh experience as we move to the making of decisions. We cannot rule it out because it is not ours; that is the error
of autocracy which insists upon the *a priori* rightness
of its own experience. We have to regard experience
as significant in itself and seek to come to terms with
it. If it is mistaken in the implication it assumes, we
have to convince it of its error. Our business, hard as
it is, is the discovery of that need in the experience
which must be satisfied if successful government is to
be possible. For successful government is simply government which satisfies the largest possible area of demand.
It is not mysterious or divine. It is simply a body of
men making decisions which, in the long run, live or
die by what other men think of them. Their validity
as decisions is in that thought if only because its content
is born of what the decisions mean to ourselves. All
of us are inescapably citizens, and, at some point,
therefore, the privacy in which we seek escape from
our obligation as citizens, will seem unsatisfying. A
crisis comes which touches us; a decision is made which
contradicts something we happen to have experienced
as fundamental; we then judge our rulers by the fact
of that denial, and act as we think its terms warrant.

This, as I think, is the real pathway to an answer
to the kind of problem which students of public opinion
like Mr. Lippmann have posed. They are right in their
analysis of the constituent factors in its making, especially
in their emphasis of the difficulties we confront in
making that opinion correspond to the realities it must
satisfy. They are right, further, I believe, in their

emphasis upon the vital connexion between truthful news and liberty; nor do I doubt that some of the remedies they propose would have the valuable effect of increasing the degree of truth in the news. But all of them, I think, miss out the vital fact that truthful news is dangerous to a society the actual contours of which its presentation might seriously change. It would have been a different war in 1914 without propaganda; the history of political parties would have been different if the principles they announced were measured by their application to total and not to partial experience. It only pays to print the truth when the interest responsible for publication is not prejudiced thereby. My point has been that in an unequal society that prejudice is inevitable.

And that prejudice, in its basic implications, is incompatible with liberty. For what it does is to emphasize some experience at the expense of other experience, to enable one need to make its way while another need remains unknown. The policy of censorship during the war meant that everyone anxious for its prosecution to the end had ample opportunity to express his view; the pacifist, the Christian, the believer in peace by negotiation, found it extraordinarily difficult to speak. Clamant opinion was, as always, taken for actual opinion; and policy, particularly in the making of peace, was built upon the assumption that no other opinion existed save that which made itself heard. To any observer with a grain of common sense, it was obvious that no treaty would be possible of application save as it impressed Germany as just, and that where, when the glow of war had gone, Germany resisted its application, a public opinion would not easily be found to demand the imposition of penalties. Nothing is more dangerous in the taking of decisions than to assume that because people are silent, they have nothing to say.

Yet that is the underlying assumption of much of our social life. We emphasize opinion which satisfies those in power, we discount opinion which runs counter to it; above all we take it for granted that silence and consent are one and the same thing. Every one of these attitudes is a blunder; especially is it a blunder, for which we pay heavily, in matters of social importance. It is extraordinarily dangerous, for example, to assume that English public opinion disapproved the General Strike because Mayfair was indignant, the *Morning Post* hysterical, and Sir John Simon coldly hostile; for Mayfair and the *Morning Post*, even with Sir John Simon, do not constitute English public opinion. Our difficulty is that they will be taken to constitute it when it is to the interest of government to do so. Such an equation is serious, and may well be fatal, to any who think of social peace as a thing really worth while to preserve.

We must remember, too, what goes along with a process of this kind. Those who lament the ignorance of public opinion too often forget that in an unequal society it is necessary to repress the expression of individuality. Every attempt at such expression is an attempt at the equalization of social conditions; it is an attempt to make myself count, an insistence on my claim, an assertion of my right to be treated as equal in that claim with other persons. To admit that I ought to have that freedom is to deny that the inequality upon which society rests is valid. And, accordingly, every sort of devious method, conscious and unconscious, is adopted to prevent my assertiveness. The most subtle, perhaps, is the denial of adequate educational facilities; for what, in fact, that does is to prevent me from knowing how to formulate my claim effectively, and inattention is the price I have to pay for my ineffectiveness. My claim, then, however real or just, because it is clumsily presented fails to secure the consideration it deserves. Or, again, the view of a group may be simply discounted where it fails to please the holders of power. We are impressed, for instance, when we hear that a government, say that of Mr. Lloyd George, is solid in its determination not to give way to the miners; we assume a careful weighing of the facts and a decision taken in the light of their total significance. But when we hear that the miners are solidly behind their leaders, we feel that this is a clear case of ignorant and misguided men being led to their destruction by agitators enjoying the exercise of power. The whole machinery of news-making is directed to the confirmation of that impression; and the chance that the miners' claim will be considered equally is destroyed by the weight which unequal economic power attaches to the case against that claim. The opinion represented by the miners is not objectively valued. It is the victim of a process of valuation the purpose of which is to prevent, so far as possible, an alteration of the *status quo*; and, *mutatis mutandis*, this is true of all claims which seek alteration in a significant degree.

Now it is, I think, unquestionable that in an unequal society, the effort of ordinary men to attain the condition we call happiness is hampered at every turn. The power of numbers is sacrificed to the interest of a few. The truth of the facts which might make a just solution is distorted for a similar end. Freedom, therefore, in an unequal society has no easy task as it seeks realization. For its search is not to realize itself for its own sake, but for what, as it is realized, it is able to bring. We seek religious freedom for the truth our religion embodies. We seek political freedom for the ends that, in the political world, we deem good. We seek economic freedom for the satisfaction brought by making an end of the frustration to our personality an

irrational subordination implies. Men do not, I believe,
resent an environment when they feel that they share
adequately in its making and in the end for which it
is made. But they are bound to be at least apathetic,
and possibly hostile, when the sense is wide and deep
that they are no more than its instruments. That is
the secret of the profound allegiance trade unionism is
able to create. Its members see in its activities the
expression of the power for which they are individually
searching. Few States—it is surely a significant thing—
have ever won from their subjects a loyalty so profound
as the Miners' Federation of Great Britain, or the
trade unions in the cotton trades. Even the blunders of
their leaders meet with a pardon far more generous
than would be extended to the political heads of the
State. The reason lies in the degree to which the trade
union expresses the intimate experience of its members.
And until the policy of the State meets that experience
with similar profundity conflict between the government
and the trade union will rarely involve the desertion
by the members of the association they have themselves
made. What the government will represent as disloyalty to the State will seem to trade unionists a service
which is freedom.

The point I am seeking to make was summarized
with the insight of genius by Disraeli when he spoke
of the rich and poor as in fact two nations. For the
poor, their voluntary organizations evoke the same
kind of impassioned loyalty as a nation struggling to be
free is able to win from its members. Anyone who
reads, for example, the early history of bodies like the
miners' unions, and seeks to measure the meaning of
the sacrifices men were willing to make on their behalf,
will realize that he is meeting precisely the same kind
of temper as he can parallel from the history of the
Italian struggle against Austria or of the Balkan fight

against Turkish domination. What Keir Hardie did for
the miners of Ayrshire, what Sidney Hillman has done
for the garment workers of America, are as epic and
as creative, in their way, as the work of Garibaldi and
Mazzini. The latter must have seemed at Vienna just
as wrong and as unwise as Keir Hardie seemed to the
mineowners fifty years ago, or Hillman to the garment
manufacturer accustomed, in the classic phrase, to
'conduct his own business in his own way'. The point
in each case is the important one that power is challenged in the interest of self-government; that the focal
point of conflict is an inability on the part of those
who govern to interpret the experience of their subjects
as these read its meaning; with the result, again in each
case, that the imposition of an interpretation from
without leaves those upon whom it is imposed with
the sense that their lives and their happiness are
instruments and not ends.

What is the outcome of it all? For me, at least,
essentially that a society pervaded by the fact of inequality is bound to deny freedom and, therefore, to
provoke conflict. Its values will be so distorted, its
apparatus for magnifying that distortion so complete,
that it is blinded to the realities which confront it. We
do not need to go far for proof. The daily newspaper,
the novel, the poet, all confirm it. Compare Macaulay's
glorification of Victorian progress with the picture in
Carlyle's *Chartism*, or Dickens's *Hard Times*. Set the
resounding complacency of Mr. Gladstone's perorations
against the indignant insight of William Morris and
Ruskin. Think of the America of President Coolidge's
speeches, and the America as bitterly described by Mr.
Sinclair Lewis. Remember that Treitschke's eulogy of
blood and iron is a picture of the same Germany as
that which Bebel and Liebknecht sought to overthrow.
Guizot's era of the *juste milieu* is the period of Proudhon

and Leroux, of Considérant and Louis Blanc, all of
them, however mistakenly, the protagonists of a just
society. Men think differently who live differently.
If we have a society of unequals, how can we agree
either about means or ends? And if this agreement is absent how can we, at least over a considerable
period, hope to move on our way in peace?

An unequal society always lives in fear, and with a
sense of impending disaster in its heart. The effect of
this atmosphere is clear enough. We have only to
examine the history of France after the death of
Louis XIV to realize exactly what it implies. Everyone
who seeks to penetrate below the surface sees some
vast calamity ahead. It may be a visitor like Chester-
field, a timid lawyer like Barbier, an ex-minister like
D'Argenson, a philosopher like Voltaire. The government itself, and those with whom it is allied, has a
perception that something new is abroad. They fear
the novelty and they seek to suppress it, in the belief
that a bold front and an adequate severity will stem
the tide of critical scepticism. But neither boldness
nor severity can stem that tide. The government falters
for a moment on the verge of concession: there is an
hour when the ministry of Turgot seemed likely to
inaugurate an era of conciliation. It is too late because
the price of conciliation is the sacrifice of precisely the
vested interests with which the government is in partnership. So the ancient régime moves relentlessly to its
destruction. It is forced to consult those whose experience it had never taken into account in the hope of
salvation; and they find that, if they are to fulfil, they
must also destroy.

That is, other things being equal, the inevitable history of such societies. Their mental habits resemble
nothing so much as the horrified timidity which persuaded Hobbes to find in despotism the only cure for

social disagreement. They are afraid of reason, for this involves an examination into their own prerogative and, as at least probable, a denunciation of the title by which it is preserved. They are afraid of concession, because they see in it an admission of the weakness of their case. They magnify scepticism into sedition and they accuse even their friends who doubt the virtue of severity of betraying the allegiance which is their due. They cannot see that men will not accept the state as the appointed conscience of the nation unless they conceive themselves to possess a full share of its benefits. They minimize the sufferings of others, because they do not have experience of them, and they magnify their own virtues that they may gain confidence in themselves. They distort history, and call it patriotism; they repress the expression of grievance and call it the maintenance of law and order. In such a society, the governors appear to their subjects as dwellers in another world; and communication between them lacks the vivifying quality of fellowship. For the truth of one party is never sufficiently the truth of another for the members to talk a common language. Every vehemence becomes a threat; and by a kind of mad logic every threat is taken as an act of treason. The society is unbalanced because justice is not its habitation. Even its generosity will be resented because it has not known how to be just.

I do not want to be taken as implying that violence is the inevitable end. I only argue that the irrefutable and inherent logic of a society where the gain of living is not proportioned to its toil is one of which violence is the inevitable end. We have never any choice in history except to follow reason wholly or, ultimately, to expect disaster; and as we approach that ultimate, the temper of the society will be what I have described. For the rule of reason in a community means that a special interest must always give way before the principles it discovers. And the rule of reason is the only kind of rule which can afford the luxury of freedom. That is, I think, because an admission that the claims of reason are paramount makes possible the emergence of a spirit of compromise. The basis of the society being just, men are not prepared for conflict over detail; but when the basis itself is unacceptable, conflict over detail is magnified into a fight over principle. In such a temper, men are always discussing with their backs on the edge of a precipice. Social discussion becomes Carlyle's ultimate question of 'Can I kill thee or canst thou kill me?' Every utterance is necessarily a challenge; and suppressed because so taken; every association is a conspiracy and attacked because so imagined. The only way to avoid so poisonous an atmosphere is to be prepared to surrender what you cannot prove it is reasonable to hold. But, human nature being what it is, men do not easily surrender what they have the power to retain; and they will pay the price of conflict if they think they can win. They do not remember that the price of conflict is the destruction of freedom and that with its loss there go the qualities which make for the humanity of men.

IV

I spoke a little earlier of the sense of national freedom; and these lectures would be even more incomplete than they are unless I sought to dwell briefly on what such freedom means. Let me take here as my text a sentence from John Stuart Mill which might well stand as the classic embodiment of one of the outstanding ideals of the nineteenth century. 'It is' he wrote, 'in general a necessary condition of free institutions that the boundaries of governments should coincide in the main with those of nationalities.' I do not need to

remind you of the commentary history has written upon
that text. In its name were accomplished the unity of
Italy and Germany, the break-up of the Turkish and
Russian empires, the separation of the Baltic peoples
from the domination of Russia. The economic motive
apart, no principle has been more fruitful of war than
the demand for national freedom. Even yet, the day
of its power is far from ended; for every misapplication
of Mill's principle in the peace treaties of 1919 has raised
problems of government which the world will find it difficult to solve without the bloody arbitrament of the sword.

Now nationality is a subjective conception that eludes
definition in scientific terms. As an Englishman, I can
feel in my bones the sense of what English nationality
implies; I feel intimately, for instance, the things that
enable me to claim Shakespeare or Jane Austen or
Dickens as typically English, without being able to
put into words the things that make them so. Every
factor to which nationality has been traced, race, language, common political allegiance, is an excessive
simplicity which betrays scientific exactitude. It is true
that nationality is born of a common historic tradition,
of achievement and suffering mutually shared; it is
true, also, that language and race, and even a common
political allegiance, have played their part in its formation. It is obvious that there is something exclusive
about nationality, that the members of any given
nation have a sense of separateness from other people
which gives them a feeling of difference, of uniqueness,
which makes domination by others so unpleasant as to
involve profound discomfort to a point which may
involve, even justly involve, resistance to that domination. But the fact remains that nationality is a psychological phenomenon rather than a juridical principle. It
is in the former, not the latter, sphere that we must
seek to meet its claims.

Mill's principle, if carried to its logical conclusion, would mean that every nation has a title to Statehood. I want you to think what that implies. The modern State is a sovereign State, and in terms of that title no will can bind its purpose but its own. The legal meaning of sovereignty is omnicompetence. The State may, as it please, make peace or war. It can erect its own tariffs, restrict its immigration, decide upon the rights of aliens within its borders, without the duty of consulting its neighbours, or paying any attention to principles of justice. States have done all these things. There is no crime they have not been prepared to commit for the defence or the extension of their own power. A different moral code has been applied in history to their acts from what we insist upon applying to individual acts, and it is, quite definitely, a lower moral code. The history of the nation which becomes a State and insists upon the prerogatives of its Statehood is a history incompatible with the terms upon which the maintenance of peace depends. That exclusive temper which, as I have argued, is the root of nationality means a measurable loss of ethical quality in those international relations which are concerned with questions of power. You have only to remember the acts which, during the war, States attempted against one another amid the applause of their subjects to realize that the recognition of national unity as a State means the destruction of private liberty and the violation of international justice, unless we can find means of setting some limit to the powers of which a nation-State can dispose.

I am particularly concerned with the exercise of those powers on their economic side. The nation-State is expected to protect the activities of its citizens outside its own boundaries. Its prestige becomes associated with its power to act in this way. So Germany supports

the Mannesman brothers in Morocco, England the
Rothschilds in Egypt, America its citizens in half the
territories of South America. Nationalism becomes
imperialism and this means the enslavement of lesser
nations to the imperialistic power. In its worst temper,
its eternal character was described by Thucydides in
that passage where he relates the tragic end of Melos,
a passage it would be mere insolence either to summarize
or to praise. Even where imperialism has resulted in
measurable benefit to the subject people, as with Great
Britain in India, or the United States in the Philippines,
the resultant loss of responsibility and character, which
an imposed rule implies, is a heavy price to pay for the
efficiency of administration that has been conferred.
The noble phrase of Sir Henry Campbell-Bannerman
that good government is no substitute for self-government seems to me borne out by every phase of the
history of imperialism. It is the imposition of a system
of experience upon a people ignorant of the character
of that experience for ends only partially its own, and
by methods which neglect unduly the relation of consent
to happiness in the process of government. The classic
case in my own experience is that of Ireland. I cannot find ground upon which to defend the habits of
Great Britain there. But those habits seem to me the
inevitable outcome of an assumption that Great Britain
was entitled to decide alone the character of her own
destiny.

Nationality, in a word, must, if it is to be consistent
with the needs of civilization, be set in the context that
matters of common interest to more than one nation-
State cannot be decided by the fiat of one member of
the international community. Modern science and
modern economic organization has reduced this world
to the unity of interdependence: the inference from this
condition is, as I think, the supremacy of cosmopolitan

need over the national claim. A nation, that is, is not
entitled to be the sole judge of its conduct where that
conduct, by its subject-matter, implicates others. It
must consult with them, compromise with them, find
the means of resolving the problem in terms of peace.
Everyone of us can think of functions that, in the
modern world, entail international consequences by
their inherent character. We have passed the stage
where we can allow a State to fix its own boundaries
as it thinks best, without consultation with other States.
The same is true of matters like the treatment of racial
minorities, of the scale of armaments, of the making of
war and peace. Everyone can see that matters like the
control of the traffic in noxious drugs, or of women
and children, of epidemics like cholera and typhus,
cannot be settled save as States co-operate upon agreed
methods of action. Most people can see, at least in
principle, that the same thing applies to labour conditions, to legal questions like the law of bills and
notes, or the rights of aliens before a municipal court,
or the incorporation of public companies. A historian
who surveyed the history of international investment
would, I think, not illegitimately conclude that there
are principles applicable to its control which can justly
regard with indifference the question of the nationality
of the investor or the State-power to which, save in
cases of default, he is certain to appeal. The importance
of the supply of raw materials to international economic
life forces us to consider the deliberate rationing of
that supply, and the maintenance of a stable world
price level which thinks first of cosmopolitan need, and,
only after a long interval, of national profit. A sane
man would, I suggest, conclude that if bodies like the
International Rail Syndicate, or the Continental Commercial Union in the glass industry, find it sensible to
transcend national competition by international agree-

ment, *a fortiori* the principle applies to matters of world-concern.

I am, of course, only illustrating the problem.[1] The principle which seems to me to emerge is the necessity for world-control where the decision is of world-concern. The inference from that principle is that the rights of the State are always subject to, and limited by, the necessarily superior rights of the international community. State-sovereignty, that is, in the sense in which the nineteenth century used that term, is obsolete and dangerous in a world like our world. It gives an authority to the nation-State which, in the light of the facts, is incompatible with the well-being of the world. It invokes the factor of prestige in realms where it has no legitimate application. It means that problems of which a wise solution is possible only in terms of reason have to find a solution amid circumstances of passion and power which obviate any possibility of justice.

For in the external, as in the internal, sphere of the State, the choice is between the use of reason and conflict. The use of reason is the law of liberty; conflict means the erosion of liberty. If States are to conduct their operations always with the knowledge in the background that the price of disagreement is war, the consequences are obvious. The atmosphere of international affairs will be poisoned by fear, and fear will bring with it the system of armaments and alliances which, in 1914, issued naturally and logically in the Great War. That was the price properly paid for a scheme of things which assumed that the legal right of the State was unlimited, and harnessed to the support of that legality every primitive and barbarous passion by which nationalism can degrade humanity. We need not be afraid to assert that, in the international sphere, the sovereignty of the State simply means the right of any

[1] Cf. my *Grammar of Politics*, Chap. XI.

powerful nation to make its own conception of self-
interest applicable to its weaker opponents. It is the
old doctrine of self-help clothed in legal form; the
doctrine against which law itself came as a protest in
the name of order and common sense. And exactly as
we cannot admit the right of a man to make his own
law in the internal life of the community, so we cannot
allow the single nation-State to make its own law in
the wider life of the international community. Because
that is what the sovereignty of the State ultimately
means, the sovereignty of the State is a conception
which outrages the patent needs of international well-
being.

I conclude, therefore, that if the nation is entitled
to self-government, it is to a self-government limited
and defined by the demands of a wider interest. I
conclude that its recognition as a State, if sovereignty
be involved in that recognition, is incompatible with
a just system of international relations. It is, further,
incompatible with the notion of an international law
regarded as binding upon the member-States of the
international community. I need not dwell upon the
impossible difficulties in which the defenders of this
doctrine have found themselves.[1] In their extreme form
they have even led a great jurist to write of war as the
supreme expression of the national will.[2] I am unable
to share such a view. Where war begins, freedom ends.
Where war begins, the opportunity of making just
solutions of any problem in dispute is indefinitely postponed. And I ask you to remember that, although,
under modern conditions, a whole nation is implicated
in war after its beginning, that is not the case either

[1] Cf. Lauterpacht, *Private Law Analogies in International Law*,
for a brilliant discussion of this question; and my paper 'Law
and the State' in *Economica*, No. 27, pp. 267 ff.
[2] Kaufman, *Das Wesen der Volkerrechts*.

with its preparation or its declaration. That is an affair
of the agents of the State whose interest in the action
they take may be totally at variance with the interest
of the people for whom they are taken as acting. They
may be serving private ambition, a particular party;
they may be acting on false information or wrong con-
ceptions. My point is that they dispose of the whole
power of the State, and that there is no means of check-
ing their activity save the very unlikely means of revolution. The full implications of national sovereignty are
a licence to wreck civilization. I cannot recognize those
implications as necessary to a proper view of national
freedom.

I deny, therefore, that there is any qualitative difference between the interests or the rights of States, and
the interests or rights of other associations or individuals.
Their purposes are ordinary, human purposes like any
other: they are a means to the happiness of their members. They have, it seems to me, to be judged by
exactly the same principles as those by which we judge
the conduct of a trade union, or a church, or a scientific
society. They do not constitute a corporate person
living on a plane different from, and having standards
other than, those of the individuals of whom they are
composed. I fully agree that no decision ought to be
taken about them, in the making of which they do not
amply share. I fully agree, also, that limitations imposed
upon their activities must pay scrupulous regard to the
psychological facts out of which they are built. I do
not, for instance, deny that the Partition of Poland was
a crime against Poland, or that its inevitable result was
to persuade millions of human beings that a war for
their resuscitation was a morally justified adventure.
But I see no difference between the Partition of Poland
and, let us say, the suppression in the community of a
Communist Party. Each seems to me an attack upon

a corporate experience which is wrong because it does not persuade those who share that experience to abandon its implications. I do not advocate the supremacy of international authority over the national State in order to destroy the national State. I advocate that supremacy as the sole way with which I am acquainted to set the great fact of nationalism in its proper perspective.

My point is, then, that the fact of a nation's existence does not entitle it to the full panoply of a sovereign State. Scotland and Wales are both of them nations; neither possesses that panoply; neither, I think, suffers in moral or psychological stature by reason of its absence. Neither, let me add, do the Scandinavian peoples—perhaps the happiest of modern communities —who are only sovereign states upon the essential condition that they do not exercise their sovereignty. But there is no more humiliation in that position than in the position any government occupies in the context of its own subjects. Power is, by its very nature, an exercise in the conditional mood. Those who exert it can only have their way by making its objects commend themselves, as, also, its methods of pursuing those objects, to those over whom it is exerted. The sovereign king in Parliament could legally disfranchise the working-classes in England; practically we know that it dare not do so. Everyone in England is aware of the grim, practical limitations under which parliamentary sovereignty operates; no one, I believe, finds humiliation in limits such as we know.

What is happening to the world is something of the same sort. The Covenant of the League of Nations is a method of limiting the unfettered exercise of national sovereign power. It is a painful and delicate operation; how painful and how delicate the timidity that has been characteristic of the League's history makes hideously

manifest. At any point in which the history of the
League is examined, elections to the Council, operations
of the Mandate system, application of a plebiscite,
resolution of an international dispute, the statesmen of
Geneva have hesitated to act upon the logic of the
world's facts. They have seen great nations confronting
them, and they have feared that those nations might,
if angered, flout the League and go their own way. So
the League has fumbled and compromised and evaded.
The big States have controlled it, and over almost all
of its history there has fallen, darkening it, the shadow
of the war.

Yet experience of the League gives us hope rather
than despair. It took three centuries to build up the
sovereign national State to that amplitude which proclaimed its own disastrous character in 1914; it would
be remarkable indeed if a decade full of memories and
hates so passionate as those of the last ten years sufficed
to overthrow its authority. We can at least say out of
the experience of those ten years that remarkable incur-
sions into that authority have occurred. We have
discovered a great range of social questions the solution
of which is not relevant to the national State or to the
problems of power that State first of all considers. We
have been able, that is, to devise subjects of government
in which national control is not the obvious technique
of operation. We have found, further, that a platform
can be constructed at Geneva the nature of which
throws any possible aggressor upon the defensive, and
suggests the possible organization against it of the rest
of the civilized world. We are finding ways of reaching
the opinion of citizens in different States over the heads
of their governments; of making those citizens demand
attention to League recommendations in a way that a
generation ago would have been unthinkable. We have
shown, and this, in some ways, is the vital discovery

of our time, that men of different nationalities can
co-operate together in the task of international government in such a way as to sink the pettiness of a narrow
outlook before the greatness of the common task. I
know that Sir Arthur Salter is a great Englishman;
but I believe his quality as an Englishman has been
made complete because he is above all a great citizen
of the world.

I do not want to exaggerate the prospects of achievement that lie before us; one blunder in Moscow or
Rome might easily destroy every hope we may tenta-
tively cherish. I want merely to note that the idea of
a world-State is slowly, painfully, hesitantly, taking
shape before our eyes. I want to emphasize the logic
of that State in an international community so inescapably interdependent as this. I want to draw therefrom the inference that national sovereignty and the
international community confront one another as
incompatibles. Even the States which have most carefully stood aloof from Geneva are in a degree to which
they are themselves unconscious within the orbit of
that influence which its idea makes so compelling.
There is hardly one aspect of the League's work in
which American citizens have not borne their share;
and I should hazard the suspicion that there have been
occasions when 'unofficial observers' have done con-
siderably more than observe unofficially. I do not
believe it is exaggeration to suggest that the underlying
motive of the Kellogg Pact was compensation by America
for her abstention from the Geneva Covenant. The
Pact, by itself, is an empty declaration; but its logic,
like that of the Covenant, is likely to take it much
further in the direction of international government
than its authors intended it should go. Even Russia,
in some sort the antipodes of Geneva, has appeared
there at Disarmament Conferences; and even granted

the rigour of the premises upon which her life is built, she cannot remain unrelated to the structure of a world-order.

I believe, accordingly, that we can retain all that is essential to the freedom of national life, and yet fully admit the implications of the international community. We can leave to England, for instance, her full cultural independence, her characteristic internal institutions, her special contacts with the Dominions she has begotten; to sacrifice the predominance of her navy, her right, by its means, to dictate the law of the sea, would still leave her England. She would still be England even if, to push speculation to the furthest point, the Suez Canal were internationalized and Gibraltar returned to Spain. France would be not the less France if the gold policy of her bank were set by an international authority, if she gave up her zeal for a conscript army, if she built her frontiers upon the impalpable solidity of friendship rather than the shifting waters of the Rhine. I can see nothing in the conceivable policy of a stronger League which would take from her the glory that has made her the Athens of the modern world. Changes in law policy, a different colonial outlook, a willingness to improve the physical standards of labour, an acceptance of naval and military forces determined upon the basis of world safety instead of national aggressiveness —it is difficult to see in any of these things such a blow at freedom as destroys the prospect of national happiness. I can see grounds for the view that an international authority which forbade the teaching of French in French schools; or altered the boundary of France so as to make Marseilles Italian; or sought the abrogation of the French civil code with its profound impact on the social customs of France; might reasonably be regarded as invading what in a nation's life that nation only can claim to decide. I can see that a nation might

feel an international authority to be oppressive if it
sought, say, by an immigration policy seriously to alter
the *mores* of a national life; it should not impose
Japanese immigration on California any more than
Great Britain seeks to impose it upon Australia. I can
even see that oppression might be felt where, in the
building of an international civil service, there was a
sense that there is discrimination against the members
of any particular nation, or that in composing the
committees of its government proper attention is not
given to the claims of some particular power.

The likelihood of any of their difficulties becoming
real is, surely, exceedingly small. An international
authority must presumably be endowed with an average
volume of human common sense; and it is no more
likely than any other authority to invite disaster. Indeed
it is rather likely to fail to embark upon experiments
and decisions it ought to make from an excessively
delicate sense of what some particular nation may feel.
International life in this realm is much more likely to
be a régime of example and influence than one of
legislative compulsion simply because the penalties of
national dissent would strain too gravely the structure
of the authority which sought an unwise imposition of
its will. Here, once more, the situation is very like that
of the internal life of a national State. There is hardly
any association the State could not overthrow if it bent
its energies to the task. But, also, most States are wise
enough to realize that victories of this kind are empty
victories, that solutions imposed by force have consequences invariably too grave to be satisfactory in their
application. Consent has its full place in the international sphere; and it is a safeguard of national right
as creative here, as elsewhere. Indeed it may reasonably
be argued that with the disappearance of national sovereignty, the factor of consent is likely to be far more

effective, far more genuinely related to the realities of
the world, than it is at the present time. For consent
between two powers like, say, America and Nicaragua,
or Great Britain and Iraq has something in it which
partakes of the ironical spirit. It is consent always in
the knowledge that refusal to agree will make no serious
difference to the result that occurs. But the surrender
of national sovereignty is the surrender of aggressive
power; and the nation can move on its way the more
freely since it knows that it no longer lives in the shadow
of international injustice.

CONCLUSION

EVERY study of freedom is a plea for toleration; and every plea for toleration is a vindication of the rights of reason. The chief danger which always confronts a society is the desire of those who possess power to prohibit ideas and conduct which may disturb them in their possession. They are rarely concerned with the possible virtues of novelty and experiment. They are interested in the preservation of a static society because in such an order their desires are more likely to be fulfilled. Their ideas of right and wrong lie at the service of those desires. The standards they formulate are nothing so much as methods of maintaining an order with which they are satisfied; and those they repress or resent, are equally methods of establishing a new order in which different demands would secure fulfilment.

But this is not a static world, and there is no means of making it so. Curiosity, discovery, invention, all of these jeopardize by their nature the foundations of any society to which their results are denied admission. Toleration is therefore not merely desirable in itself, but also politically wise, because no other atmosphere of activity offers the assurance of peaceful adjustment. If power is held by a few, happiness will be confined to a few also. Every novelty will seem a challenge to that confinement; and it will always accrete about itself the wills of those who are excluded from a share in its benefits. For this world is not only dynamic; it is also diverse. The path to happiness is not a single one. Men are not willing to yield the insight of their experience to other men's insight merely because they are

207

commanded to do so. They must be persuaded by reason that one vision of desire is better than another vision, the experience commended to them must persuade and not enforce, if they are to accept its implications with a sense of contentment.

This is, of course, a counsel of perfection. Men enjoy the exercise of power; no passion has a deeper hold upon human impulse. The willingness to admit the prospect of difference, the courage to see that one's private truth is never commensurate with the whole truth, these are the rarest of human qualities. That is why the friends of liberty are always a minority in every society. That is why, also, the maintenance of liberty is a thing that has to be fought for afresh every day, lest an inert acceptance of some particular imposition make the field of action accessible to a general tyranny. For it is impossible to confine the area in which freedom may be permitted to some special and defined part of conduct. Those who have fought for the right to think freely in theology or the natural sciences are not less certainly the ancestors of political freedom. Without Bruno and Galileo there would have been neither Rousseau nor Voltaire.

Liberty, therefore, cannot help being a courage to resist the demands of power at some point that is deemed decisive; and, because of this, liberty, also, is an inescapable doctrine of contingent anarchy. It is always a threat to those who operate the engines of authority that prohibition of experience will be denied. It is always an assertion that he who has learned from life some lesson he takes to be truth will seek to live that lesson unless he can be persuaded of its falsehood. Punishment may persuade some to abandon the effort; and others may be driven by its imposition to conceal their impulse to act upon the view they take. But persecution, however thoroughgoing, will never, over any long period, be able to suppress significant truth. If the principles that are urged by a few correspond to some widespread experience those who recognize the expression of their experience will inevitably reaffirm it. It has been the historic character of persecution always to degrade the persecutor and to strengthen the persecuted by drawing attention to their claims. The only way to deal with novelty is to understand it, and the only way to deal with grievance is to seek a remedy for the complaint it embodies. To deny novelty or grievance a right of expression is a certain, if, indeed, an ultimate, validation of the truth they contain.

We have, it appears, to learn this anew in each generation. We grant toleration in one part of the field only to deny it in another. We grant it in religion to deny it in politics; we grant it in politics, to deny it in economic matters. Each age finds that the incidence of freedom is significant at some special point, and there, once more, the lesson of freedom has to be learned. Each age makes some idol in its own image and sacrifices upon its altar the freedom of those who refuse it worship. Ultimately, that denial is always made upon the same ground: it is insisted that the doctrines or practices attacked are subversive of the civil order. The intolerance may be Catholic, when it insists that a unity of outlook is essential for the preservation of society; or it may be Protestant when, as with Calvin and the Socinians, it holds that the blasphemous nature of the belief anathematized destroys the reverence upon which society depends. The essence of the persecuting position is always that the persecutor has hold of truth and that he would betray its service by allowing it to be questioned. He is able, accordingly, to indulge in the twofold luxury not only of preserving his own authority, but also of assisting the persons attacked to enter if they so choose, the way of truth.

When attacks on liberty are political or economic, it is their motive rather than their nature that changes. A political pattern has the same hold upon its votaries as a religion; the enthusiasts of Moscow and of Rome differ only in the object of their worship. An economic system defends itself in just the same way: the devotees of Marxism in its extreme form have never doubted their right to impose their outlook upon the recalcitrant, even at the cost of blood. In a constitutional state like America the suppression of liberty is called the inhibition of licence; in a dictatorship like Moscow it is termed resistance to the admission of incorrect 'bourgeois' notions. Always the effort is to insist upon an artificial unity the maintenance of which is necessary to the desires of those who hold power. Suppression, doubtless, eases the way of authority, for scepticism is always painful, and to arrive at a conclusion after careful testing of evidence always involves the possibility that authority may have to admit that its conclusions are mistaken.

Yet it may still be maintained with some confidence that the only adequate answer to a principle which claims social recognition is the rational proof that it is untrue. It may even be argued that the world would be a happier world if this were the general theory underlying the activities of society. Civilization is strewn with the wrecks of systems which men at one time held for true; systems, also, in the name of which liberty was denied and pain needlessly inflicted. A scrutiny of history, moreover, makes it plain that the right to liberty will always be challenged where its consequence is the equalization of some privilege which is not generally shared by men. The more consciously, therefore, we can seek that equalization as a desirable object of social effort, the more likely we are to make attacks upon liberty more rare, the evil results of such attack less frequent. No man's love of justice is strong enough to survive the right to inflict punishment in the name of the creed he professes; and the simplest way to retain his sense of justice is to take away the interest which persuades him of the duty to punish. Scepticism, it may be, is a dissolvent of enthusiasm; but enthusiasm has always been the enemy of freedom. The atmosphere we require, if we are to attain happiness for the multitude, is one in which we have everything to gain by the statement of experience and nothing to lose by the investigation of its convictions. That atmosphere is the condition of liberty and its quality is light rather than heat. For light permits of argument, and we cannot argue with men who are in a passion. Nothing is so likely to engender passion as the perception that they are called to sacrifice a privilege. The way, therefore, of freedom is to arrange the pattern of social institutions so that there are no privileges to sacrifice.

This kind of plea for liberty is built, after all, upon the simple consideration that the world is likely to be the more happy if it refuses to build its institutions upon injustice. And institutions are necessarily unjust if the impression they continually produce in the majority is a feeling of envy and hatred for the results they impose. There is something wrong in a system which, like ours, maintains itself not by the respect and affection it evokes, but by the sanctions to which it can appeal. What is wrong in them is their erection upon the basis of passion and their insistence that reason shall serve what that passion is seeking to protect. So long as that is true of our society, we shall continue to deny the validity of all principles which attack the existing disposition of social forces. Those principles may often be wrong; yet sometimes, at least, they represent the certainties of the future. It is always a hazardous enterprise to suppress belief which claims to be rooted in the experience of men.

For no outlook which has behind it the support of considerable numbers will ever silently acquiesce in its reduction to impotence. It will fight for its right to be heard whatever the price of the conflict. Here it has been urged that conflict of this kind is usually unnecessary and frequently disastrous. It has been claimed that truth can be established by reason alone; that departure from the way of reason as a method of securing conviction is an indication always of a desire to protect injustice. Where there is respect for reason, there, also, is respect for freedom. And only respect for freedom can give final beauty to men's lives.

Complete list of all Penguin and Pelican Books to the end of 1937

N B

NEW BOOKS MAY HAVE BEEN
ADDED TO THE SERIES SINCE
THIS BOOK WAS PRINTED. ASK
YOUR BOOKSELLER FOR THE
LATEST LIST

Penguin Books Limited

HARMONDSWORTH MIDDLESEX

ENGLAND

PENGUIN BOOKS

COMPLETE LIST OF PUBLICATIONS TO THE END OF 1937

FICTION   *orange covers*

CRIME FICTION   green covers

61 THE MYSTERIOUS AFFAIR AT STYLES by Agatha Christie

62 THE MISSING MONEYLENDER by W. Stanley Sykes

64 THE FOUR JUST MEN by Edgar Wallace

65 THE MAN IN THE DARK by John Ferguson

78 TRENT'S LAST CASE by E. C. Bentley

79 THE RASP by Philip Macdonald

89 THE DOCUMENTS IN THE CASE by Dorothy L. Sayers
(with Robert Eustace)

90 THE SANFIELD SCANDAL by Richard Keverne

98 THE MURDERS IN PRAED STREET by John Rhode

101 MR. JUSTICE RAFFLES by E. W. Hornung

111 THE HOUND OF THE BASKERVILLES by A. Conan Doyle

TRAVEL & ADVENTURE   *cerise covers*

60 THE DARK INVADER by Captain von Rintelen

66 THE SURGEON'S LOG by J. Johnston Abraham

67 MY SOUTH SEA ISLAND by Eric Muspratt

68 WITH MYSTICS AND MAGICIANS IN TIBET by Alexandra David-Neel

69 } SOME EXPERIENCES OF A NEW GUINEA RESIDENT
70 }   MAGISTRATE by C. A. W. Monckton (in two volumes)

82 UNDERTONES OF WAR by Edmund Blunden

99 } THE WORST JOURNEY IN THE WORLD : ANTARCTIC
100 }   1910–1913 by Apsley Cherry-Garrard (in two volumes)

113 THE SECRET OF THE SAHARA by Rosita Forbes

BIOGRAPHY & MEMOIRS   *dark blue covers*

1 ARIEL by André Maurois

7 TWENTY-FIVE by Beverley Nichols

71 CONFESSIONS AND IMPRESSIONS by Ethel Mannin

77 GREY WOLF : MUSTAFA KEMAL by H. C. Armstrong

110 DISRAELI by André Maurois

114 } FOCH : MAN OF ORLEANS by B. H. Liddell Hart (in two
115 }   volumes)

NOVEMBER 1937:

116 ON ENGLAND by Stanley Baldwin
117 SEVEN FAMOUS ONE-ACT PLAYS
118 WHILE ROME BURNS by Alexander Woollcott
119 BILLIARDS AND SNOOKER FOR AMATEUR PLAYERS by
      Horace Lindrum
120 PENGUIN PARADE (I) New Stories by contemporary writers

JANUARY 1938:

121 LEAN MEN by Ralph Bates
122 LORD OF ARABIA by H. C. Armstrong
123 SOLDIERS' PAY by William Faulkner
124 IT WALKS BY NIGHT by John Dickson Carr
125 AN INDIAN DAY by Edward Thompson
126 TRADER HORN by Alfred Aloysius Horn
127 THE HAVERING PLOT by Richard Keverne
128 WINGED WARFARE by W. A. Bishop
129 ⎱ THE NONESUCH WEEK-END BOOK
130 ⎰   (in two volumes)

PELICAN BOOKS *light blue covers*

A series of books on science, economics, history, sociology, archaeology, etc. Edited by V. K. Krishna Menon ;—*advisory editors* : H. L. Beales, Reader in Economic History, University of London ; W. E. Williams, Secretary, the British Institute of Adult Education ; Sir Peter Chalmers-Mitchell, Secretary of the Zoological Society, London, 1903–35.

A 1 ⎫ THE INTELLIGENT WOMAN'S GUIDE TO SOCIALISM,
A 2 ⎬ CAPITALISM, SOVIETISM AND FASCISM by Bernard
   ⎭ Shaw (in two volumes)

A 3 LAST AND FIRST MEN by Olaf Stapledon

A 4 DIGGING UP THE PAST by Sir Leonard Woolley (*with 32 half-tone plates*)

A 5 A SHORT HISTORY OF THE WORLD by H. G. Wells (*with numerous maps*)

A 6 PRACTICAL ECONOMICS by G. D. H. Cole (*first publication*)

A 7 ESSAYS IN POPULAR SCIENCE by Julian Huxley (*illustrated*)

A 8 THE FLOATING REPUBLIC by Dobrée and Manwaring (*The mutinies at the Nore and Spithead in 1797*)

A 9 A HISTORY OF THE ENGLISH PEOPLE (I) by Elie Halévy

A 10 THE MYSTERIOUS UNIVERSE by Sir James Jeans (*with 2 half-tone plates*)

A 11 THE GREAT VICTORIANS (I) edited by H. J. and Hugh Massingham

A 12 THE INEQUALITY OF MAN by J. B. S. Haldane

A 13 LIBERTY IN THE MODERN STATE by Harold J. Laski (*with new introduction*)

A 14 SOCIAL LIFE IN THE INSECT WORLD by J. H. Fabre (*with 15 half-tone plates*)

A 15 THE GROWTH OF CIVILISATION by W. J. Perry (*with several maps*)

A 16 A HISTORY OF THE ENGLISH PEOPLE (II) by Elie Halévy

A 17 A BOOK OF ENGLISH POETRY collected by G. B. Harrison (*a new anthology*)

A 18 AFTER THE DELUGE by Leonard Woolf

A 19 MEDIEVAL PEOPLE by Eileen Power (*with 8 half-tone plates*)

A 20 VISION AND DESIGN by Roger Fry

More titles to follow.

THE PENGUIN SHAKESPEARE

A sixpenny Shakespeare specially edited for Penguin Books by Dr. G. B. Harrison. Each volume contains a chronological list of Shakespeare's works, a short life of Shakespeare, a note on the Elizabethan Theatre with a drawing, a brief Introduction to the Play, a Glossary and an Index. All this material is completely new. The following plays have already been issued:

B 1 TWELFTH NIGHT	B 7 THE TEMPEST
B 2 HAMLET	B 8 THE MERCHANT OF VENICE
B 3 HENRY THE FIFTH	
B 4 KING LEAR	B 9 RICHARD II
B 5 AS YOU LIKE IT	B 10 ROMEO AND JULIET
B 6 A MIDSUMMER NIGHT'S DREAM	B 11 JULIUS CAESAR
	B 12 MACBETH

Other volumes to follow shortly.

If you have any suggestions to make for future books, please don't hesitate to send them in.